English

A LINGUARAMA
REFERENCE GUIDE

BOOK 2

First edition 1995
Revised edition 1996
Reprinted 1997
Reprinted 1998
Reprinted 1999 (twice)
Reprinted 2000 (twice)
Reprinted 2001
Revised edition 2002
Reprinted 2003
Revised edition 2004

Linguarama Publications
Oceanic House
89 High Street
Alton
Hants GU34 1LG

ISBN 0 906256 37 2

Printed in Great Britain
by Nuffield Press, Abingdon, Oxon

© Linguarama Publications

Contents

Grammar

Verbs: Present, Past and Future

1.	Present Simple	(I work)	2
2.	Present Continuous	(I am working)	8
3.	Past Simple	(I worked)	14
4.	Past Continuous	(I was working)	18
5.	Used to and Would		22
6.	Present Perfect Simple	(I have worked)	26
7.	Present Perfect Continuous	(I have been working)	32
8.	Past Perfect Simple	(I had worked)	36
9.	Past Perfect Continuous	(I had been working)	40
10.	Going to		44
11.	Will		48

Verbs: Passive

12.	Passive	56

Verbs: Conditionals

13.	Conditionals (If): Introduction	60
14.	Conditional 0	64
15.	Conditional 1	66
16.	Conditional 2	68
17.	Conditional 3	72

Verbs: Infinitive and Gerund

18.	Infinitive	([To] work)	74
19.	Gerund (...ing)	(Working)	80

Modal Verbs

20.	Introduction	84
21.	Will and Would	88
22.	Can and Could	92
23.	May and Might	98
24.	Must and Have to	102
25.	Needn't and Mustn't	106
26.	Shall and Should	112
27.	Ought to	116

Adjectives and Adverbs

28.	Adjectives and Adverbs	118
29.	Frequency Adverbs	124
30.	Comparatives and Superlatives	126

Clauses

31.	Reported Speech	132
32.	Time Clauses	138
33.	Relative Clauses	142

Prepositions

34.	Introduction	146
35.	Verbs + Prepositions	148
36.	Nouns + Prepositions	154
37.	Prepositions + Nouns	158

Nouns

38.	Countable and Uncountable Nouns	164

Determiners

39.	Articles (a/an/the)	168
40.	Some and Any	172
41.	Quantity (How Much?)	176
42.	Both, Neither, Either	182
43.	Each and Every	186

Easily Confused Words

44.	Make or Do?	188
45.	Rise or Raise?	190
46.	When or If?	192
47.	So or Such?	194

General Information

48.	Time	196
49.	The Diary	198
50.	Numbers	200
51.	British and American Grammar Differences	204
52.	Common Problems	206

Everyday Communication

53.	Greetings and Farewells	216
54.	Introductions	220
55.	Socialising: Polite Phrases	224
56.	Socialising: Asking Other People	232
57.	Reacting	236
58.	Comparing and Contrasting	240
59.	Connecting Ideas	242
60.	Describing Trends	246
61.	Expressing Certainty, Probability and Possibility	252
62.	Forecasting	254
63.	Generalising	255
64.	Persuading and Recommending	256
65.	Sequencing	258
66.	Help! (What to Say When You Have a Problem)	261

Business Skills

Telephoning

67.	Introduction	265
68.	Getting Through	266
69.	Problems Getting Through	274

Presentations

70.	Structure	279
71.	Getting Started	280
72.	The Main Part	284
73.	The Final Part	290
74.	Dealing With Questions	294

Meetings

75.	Structure	299
76.	Chairing a Meeting	300
77.	Controlling the Meeting	304
78.	Participating in a Meeting	310
79.	The End of the Meeting	318

Negotiations

80.	Structure	321
81.	Getting Started	322
82.	The Discussion Phase	328
83.	Proposing and Bargaining	334
84.	The Final Part	340

Writing

85.	Letter and E-mail Writing	344
86.	Form Filling	351
87.	Report Writing	352

Words at Work

88.	Introduction	360
89.	Companies	364
90.	Production	368
91.	Sales	372
92.	Marketing	374
93.	Advertising	378
94.	Finance	382
95.	Personnel (Human Resources)	390

Reference

96.	Irregular Verbs	396

Index

399

Introduction

About this book

"English 2: a Linguarama Reference Guide" is designed for use after a course, or for self-study. It will help you to consolidate, revise, and practise the English that you have learnt. English 2 is at a higher level than English 1.

The book is divided into four sections:

Grammar

Each unit deals with an important aspect of grammar which is illustrated by examples, clear explanations of its use, and a table or diagram which displays the form of the particular grammatical structure. There is a unit on common areas of difficulty.

Everyday Communication

This section gives examples of useful everyday language that can be used in social and business situations and also points out which phrases are formal and which are informal.

Business Skills

In this section, you can find useful language for business activities such as telephoning, letter and report writing, making presentations and taking part in meetings and negotiations.

Words at Work

Useful items of business vocabulary are included in this section. British and American differences have been highlighted.

There is a separate work book containing self-study exercises corresponding to the units in this book.

How can you use this book?

For reference
The Linguarama Reference Guide can be used simply as a reference book with which you can remind yourself of a useful piece of language for a particular purpose.

You may, for example, be writing something in English and feel unsure about a certain grammar point. You can look this up in the *contents list* or *index* and then look at the example sentences in the unit. Or, you may be preparing to make a presentation and wish to check some of the phrases you need to use when referring to visual information. There is a helpful list in the book. When you are about to make a telephone call, look at the relevant section: leaving messages in case the person you are calling is not in the office, for example, may be just the language you need to remind yourself of.

For self-study
Decide which piece of language you wish to revise. For example, do you find the use of the Present Perfect tense difficult? Before opening the book, note down the ways in which you think it is used and write some example sentences. After that, look at the unit in the book to check your understanding. Read the examples in the unit and look carefully at any notes or possible problem areas.

Checklist
Keep a checklist of the mistakes you make frequently and the correct version. This will help you to be aware of which aspects of language you need to revise.

Symbols used in this book

This indicates common problems and important points.

This refers the reader to another chapter or chapters with relevant information.

Flags show the differences between:

British   and   American usage.

In the grammar section:

indicates the positive (affirmative) form of verbs.

—

indicates the negative form of verbs.

indicates the question form of verbs.

We acknowledge, with thanks, the contribution of Anne Laws to the preparation of this book.

Grammar

1 Present Simple (I work)

Routines

> To achieve quality control, staff **meet** regularly and **review** all the work in their department. The sales managers **have** frequent meetings with customers and **discuss** any problems. We **set** targets for improving our quality standards.

Other examples

I sometimes **listen** to my car radio on the way to work.
The Personnel Manager **carries out** staff appraisals once a year.
We usually **hold** our meetings at Head Office in London.
We hardly ever **have** conferences in Paris these days.
I always **play** tennis with a friend on Sundays.

I **don't** often **have** time to read the newspaper. I**'m** too busy.
John **doesn't** usually **attend** the sales meetings.

How often **do** you **visit** the warehouse?
Does your company **publish** a quarterly report?

Note

Adverbs of frequency (always, often, sometimes, never, usually, etc.) are often used with the Present Simple.

See *Frequency Adverbs* (Unit 29).

HOW OFFEN?

They **meet**...

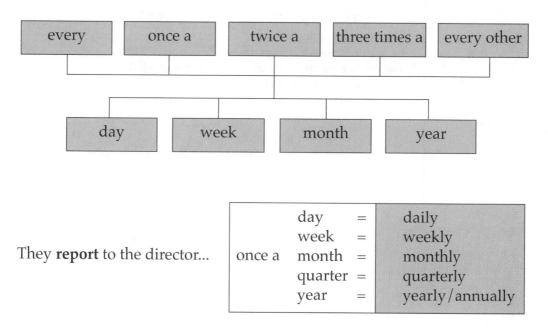

They **report** to the director... once a
day	=	daily
week	=	weekly
month	=	monthly
quarter	=	quarterly
year	=	yearly/annually

General facts/truths

> The Kamatsu Company **produces** a wide range of computer hardware. It **has** plants in fifteen countries round the world. Its main markets **are** in the Far East but it also **sells** in Europe and the United States.

Other examples

Klaus Stein **lives** near Frankfurt and **works** for one of the major German banks in the city.

My company **operates** in over twenty countries around the world.

Water **boils** at 100 degrees centigrade.

I **don't deal** with routine enquiries. My assistant **deals** with those.

Jane **doesn't work** in the London office any more. She has moved to Birmingham.

How many people **does** your company **employ**?

VERBS: PRESENT, PAST AND FUTURE

Measurement

We use the Present Simple to talk about measurement.

The parcel **weighs** one kilo.
How much **does** this **cost**, please?
The room **measures** six metres by four and a half metres.
The car **costs** a thousand dollars to produce.
The film **lasts** one hour.

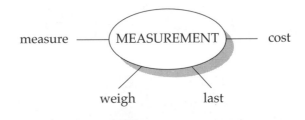

Opinions, perceptions and states

Our contractors **don't like** our proposals for completing the work more quickly. They say we **don't understand** their problems. They **seem** to think it's unnecessary to change the plans. They **doubt** whether the work will be finished before the end of next month.

Other examples

Could you phone Mr. Brown's assistant about the meeting next week? I **forget** her name, but you **know** who I **mean**.
Heinrich **wants** to buy a sports car.
I **hate** walking when there's snow on the ground.
We have several different ideas for a new product but we haven't decided yet which is best. It **depends** on the results of the market research.

Do you **remember** Mary's telephone number?
What **do** you **think** of the new five-year plan?
Who **does** this coat **belong** to?

STATIVE VERBS

Some verbs (opinions, perceptions and states) are normally used in the Present Simple tense (and not in the Present Continuous). We call these verbs (that express states or perceptions, *not* actions), Stative Verbs.

Stative Verbs

Opinions

dislike
hate
like
love
prefer
think

Knowledge & Perception

believe
doubt
forget
hope
know
remember
seem
suppose
understand

Other States

belong
contain
depend
hear
mean
need
own
require
see
want

Think and See

Think: When it **expresses an opinion**, 'think' is only used in the Simple form:

I **think** it's a good idea.

When it means **'consider something before making a decision'**, it can be used in the Continuous form:

I**'m thinking** of going to Greece for my holiday.

See: 'See' is normally only used in the Simple form:

I **see** what you mean.

However, when it means **'meet'**, it can be used in the Continuous form:

He**'s seeing** his brother on Saturday.

! Typical Errors	Correct
I am not remembering his name. Peter Spencer is owning most of the shares in the company. The rest are belonging to members of his family. I am believing that you are right.	I **don't remember** his name. Peter Spencer **owns** most of the shares in the company. The rest **belong** to members of his family. I **believe** that you are right.

Future schedules

The train **leaves** at ten and **arrives** at twelve.
The meeting **begins** at one o'clock.

**SALES MEETING
BIRMINGHAM
JANUARY 8**

10.00   Train departs
         Euston Station

12.00   Arrive Birmingham

13.00   Meeting starts

18.00   Leave Birmingham

Other examples

What time **does** the train **leave**?
What time **does** the meeting **begin**?

We **don't leave** until six o'clock.

The film **ends** at ten thirty.
The game **starts** at two o'clock.
We **arrive** in Edinburgh at eleven and then **visit** the castle.

PRESENT SIMPLE

+	I/we/you/they	work
	he/she/it	works

−	I/we/you/they	do not (don't)	work
	he/she/it	does not (doesn't)	

?	Do	I/we/you/they	work?
	Does	he/she/it	

2 Present Continuous (I am working)

Something happening at the time of speaking

"Hello, Peter. What **are** you **doing**?"
"**I'm looking** at the report on the new stock control system. It**'s taking** longer than I expected. It's very badly written."

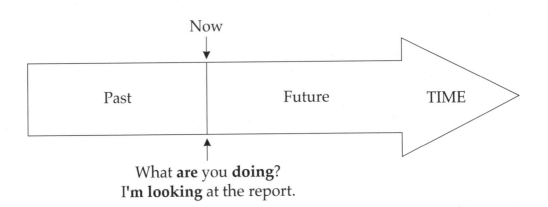

What **are** you **doing**?
I'm looking at the report.

Other examples

"Can I see you in my office, Jackie?"
"Yes. I'll be with you in a minute. **I'm** just **faxing** this letter to the Managing Director."

"Who **is** Paul **talking** to?"
"That's the new accounts clerk."

I'm not making much progress with this spreadsheet. Can you help me?

What's wrong with these fax machines? This one **isn't working.** The ones downstairs **aren't working** either. **Is** anyone **doing** anything about it?

Something happening around the time of speaking

> Heinz **isn't doing** any work on the research project this week. He**'s attending** the sales conference.

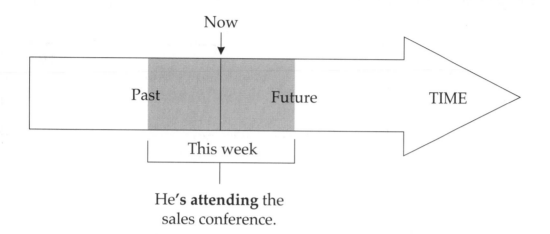

He**'s attending** the sales conference.

Other examples

They **are installing** some new machinery in the factory this month.
The marketing department **are preparing** a new version of the company brochure.
My daughter**'s learning** to drive.
George **is helping** to set up the new branch in Scotland.

"**Are** you still **working** on that project, Tom?"
"Yes, I **am**." (*He may not be doing this **exactly** at the time of speaking.*)

Changing situations

> The company **is making** a loss because costs **are rising** and sales **are falling.**

Other examples

Unemployment figures **are rising** rapidly.
Mario's English **is improving** all the time.
The company **is growing** fast.
The world climate **is changing**. The polar ice cap **is shrinking**.

VERBS: PRESENT, PAST AND FUTURE

Future arrangements

> The Sales Manager **is flying** to Rome on Monday. John**'s picking** him up at the airport at 11.00 and he**'s meeting** Mr Ferrero at 2.00.

March	March
Sunday 1	**Thursday 5**
	~~London Meeting~~
Monday 2	**Friday 6**
Rome: arrive 11.00	
Mr Ferrero 14.00	
Tuesday 3	**Saturday 7**
Press Conference 10.30	*Football 15.00*
Shareholders' Meeting 15.00	
Wednesday 4	**Notes**
Production Meeting 10.30	
Lunch with supplier 13.00	

Other examples

We**'re holding** a press conference on Tuesday morning, and then we**'re having** a meeting of the shareholders in the afternoon.

I'll be in the office on Thursday. We**'re not having** a meeting in London after all. It has been postponed.

"**Are** you **seeing** the Production Manager this week?"
"Yes, I**'m meeting** him on Wednesday morning, and afterwards we**'re having** lunch with the new supplier."

"**Are** you **coming** to the barbecue on Saturday?"
"No, I'm afraid I can't. I**'m taking** my children to a football match."

Present Simple or Present Continuous?

> "Where **do** you **live**, Mary?"
> "Well, I normally **live** and **work** in London but as **I'm helping** out in one of our branches at the moment, **I'm staying** with friends in the country."
> "**Do** you often **do** that? **Move** around from branch to branch?"
> "Not very often."

Contrasting examples

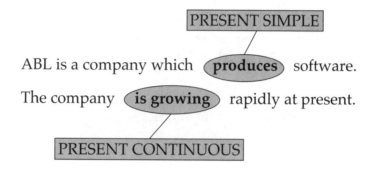

PRESENT SIMPLE	PRESENT CONTINUOUS
Normal activity (generally, usually, always)	**Temporary activity** (now, at the moment)
He **works** for Fiat in Milan.	He**'s having** a holiday in the UK at the moment.
They **check** the stock once a month.	They **are checking** the stock at the moment.
She **doesn't** normally **work** in the sales office. She **works** in accounts.	She**'s working** in the sales office at present.
Most children **learn** a foreign language at school.	He**'s learning** French.
I usually **write** the monthly reports.	I**'m not working** on the report at the moment.

⚠ Typical Errors	Correct
~~I am living in Britain.~~	I **live** in Britain.
~~I work on this report at the moment.~~	I **am working** on this report at the moment.

Emphasizing very frequent action

> He**'s** always **phoning** me at midnight.

Other examples
English people **are** always **apologising**.
This train **is** always **running** late.

Always is normally used with the Present Simple:
I always **play** football on Saturdays.
He always **gives** his assistant a present at Christmas.

When the Present Continuous is used for very frequent actions, it suggests that the speaker is rather angry or finds the situation strange.
He**'s always forgetting** to lock the door when he leaves. (*This annoys me.*)
My car **is always breaking down**. (*This annoys me.*)
She**'s always eating** chocolate bars. (*I find this strange.*)

PRESENT CONTINUOUS

+	I	am ('m)	working
	he/she/it	is ('s)	
	we/you/they	are ('re)	

−	I	am not ('m not)	working
	he/she/it	is not (isn't)	
	we/you/they	are not (aren't)	

?	Am	I	working?
	Is	he/she/it	
	Are	we/you/they	

VERBS: PRESENT, PAST AND FUTURE

3 Past Simple (I worked)

A past activity or situation

> Sedco **announced** record profits last week. Sales **were** up by twenty-five per cent. Turnover **rose** to fifty million. The company **increased** its share of the market by three per cent.

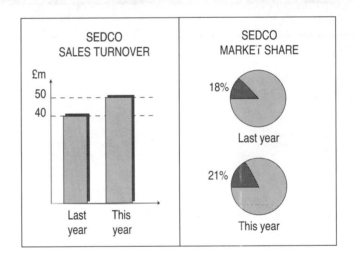

Regular verbs

I didn't send the report out yesterday because I **wanted** to make some changes to it.

Last year, the company **developed** a new product which was highly successful.

I **discussed** the plans with Peter last week as I **wanted** his comments.

When **did** you **decide** to appoint a new assistant?

"When **did** you **start** your present job?"
"I **joined** the company in 1980 when I **graduated** from university."

Irregular verbs

I **saw** Jim yesterday. He **told** me he'd be late for the meeting tomorrow.
The negotiations **began** last month but they **broke down** after only a few days.

Did Geoff **bring** my book back yesterday? I **lent** it to him ages ago and it's time he **brought** it back.

When you **saw** Bill, **did** you **tell** him about that memo from Head Office?

I **thought** I should check the letter before it **went** out. I **didn't know** whether John had checked it. I **was** right, I **came** across a few mistakes.

Note

Most regular verbs end in '-d' or '-ed' in the Past Simple. Irregular verbs do not.

See the list of *Irregular Verbs* (Unit 96).

Useful time phrases with the past

I knew him when I worked in Sweden **ten years ago**.

Other examples

The previous meeting was held in Barcelona **last month.**
We got married **when** we lived in Hong Kong.
I haven't seen him since the Paris conference and that was **ages ago.**
Dr. Jorgensen joined the company **in 1990**.

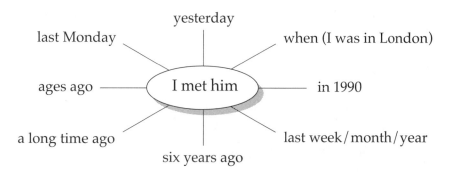

VERBS: PRESENT, PAST AND FUTURE

Polite requests

> I **wondered** if you could help me with this translation.

Other examples

I **wanted** to ask you a question.
I **wanted** to ask you a favour.
I **wondered** if you could give me some advice about which computer to buy.

*We can also use the **Present Simple** in requests:*
I **wonder** if you **can** help me? (= *request*)

*The use of the Past Simple in these requests makes them very polite. (We are **not** talking about past time!)*
I **wondered** if you **could** help me? (= *very polite request*)

Expressing wishes

> I wish I **had** a bigger car.

Other examples

I wish we **had** more time to plan this project.
Jack wished he **was** a better rugby player.

Note

*Although we often use the Past Simple for wishes, we are not talking about past time. The meaning is **"I would like..."**, e.g. "I **would like** to have more free time".*

We can also say:

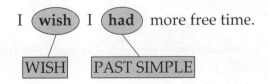

Referring to the future (it's time...)

It's time the children **were** in bed.

Other examples

It's high time we **started** the meeting.
It's eleven o'clock already. It's time we **went** home.

Note

*The Past Simple can be used with **'it's time'** to talk about the future.* **"It's time we went home"** *means* **"It's time to go home"**. *'It's high time' makes it stronger, more urgent.*

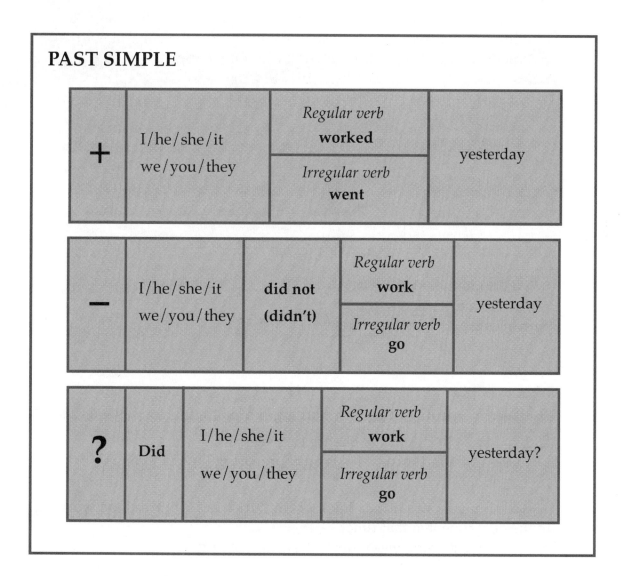

4 Past Continuous
(I was working)

At a particular time in the past

> I'd like to talk about the department's achievements over the past year. At this time last year, we **were wondering** whether the department would be closed down. Fortunately, this did not happen.

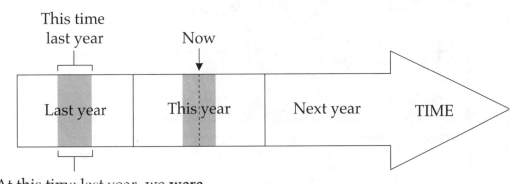

At this time last year, we **were wondering** whether the department would be closed down.

Other examples

What **were** you **doing** yesterday morning? I tried to ring you several times.

"Did you go to the Milan conference last week, Jim?"
"No, I didn't, unfortunately. I **was** busy **preparing** for an important presentation."

"The company moved its headquarters to Zürich in 1990. **Was** John **working** in the department at that time?"
"No, he **was finishing** his engineering course at university."

With the Past Simple

Heinz **was working** for Mercedes Benz when the company **merged** with Daimler.

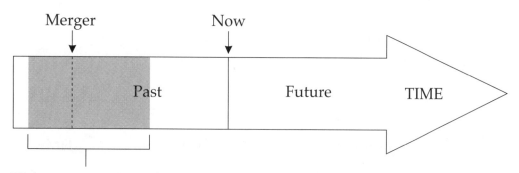

Heinz **was working** for Mercedes Benz when the companies **merged**.

Other examples

I **met** my wife when I **was working** in Milan.
John's car **broke** down when he **was driving** to London.
We **were thinking** of moving to a bigger house when my husband **lost** his job.

"**Were** you **speeding** when the accident **happened**?"
"No, I **wasn't**. I **was** only **doing** thirty."

Note

We use the Past Simple for the shorter action which interrupts the longer action (Past Continuous).

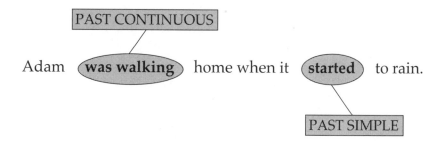

The Past Continuous is often used with ***'when'***.

VERBS: PRESENT, PAST AND FUTURE

Continuous actions happening at the same time

> We had a lot of enquiries in response to the advertisement for the job vacancy. My assistant **was answering** calls all last week while I **was interviewing** candidates.

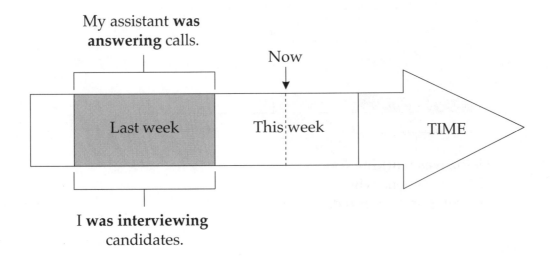

Other examples

"You and James were both very busy yesterday. What **were** you **doing**?"
"James **was organising** deliveries from the warehouse while I **was** out **visiting** some clients."

While I **was finishing** the training course, I **was** also **looking** for a job.
I **was negotiating** a new contract in Paris while my boss **was attending** a meeting in Madrid.

Note
While = at the same time

PAST CONTINUOUS

+	I/he/she/it	was	working
	we/you/they	were	

−	I/he/she/it	was not (wasn't)	working
	we/you/they	were not (weren't)	

?	Was	I/he/she/it	working?
	Were	we/you/they	

5 Used to and Would

Used to

> He **used to** work for Deutsche Bank. He's with the Dresdner now.

Other examples

I **used to** play a lot of tennis when I was younger, but I don't have so much time now.

Ian **used to** live in London but he moved to Brussels last year.

We **used to** have a subsidiary in France but we sold it five years ago.

The company **didn't use to** manufacture this type of product, but the demand was there so we decided to meet it.

Didn't Paul **use to** smoke?

I'm sure I've met you somewhere before. **Did** you **use to** attend the sales meetings in Italy?

Note

'Used to' is for situations or states that happened regularly in the past but which no longer happen:

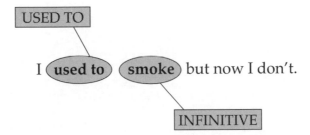

22   GRAMMAR

Do not confuse 'I used to' with 'I am used to + ...ing'.

I have been living in England for five years now and I **am used to eating** English food.
(I am accustomed to eating English food. I don't think it is strange because I have been doing it for a long time.)

Would

> She worked very hard when she was in Germany. She **would** stay in the office until eight o'clock every evening.

Other examples

The Sales Manager used to have a meeting every week and **would** get very angry if anyone was late.

When we were on holiday, we used to get up early and we**'d** play tennis for two hours before breakfast.

'Would' cannot be used to show changes between the past and the present.

! Typical Error	Correct
~~I would work for Esso (but now I don't).~~	I **used to** work for Esso (but now I don't).

VERBS: PRESENT, PAST AND FUTURE

*Be careful with word order when a sentence includes an **adverb of frequency**, (e.g. always, usually, often, sometimes, never).*

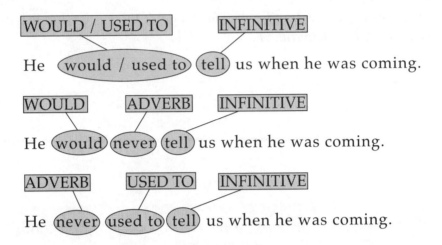

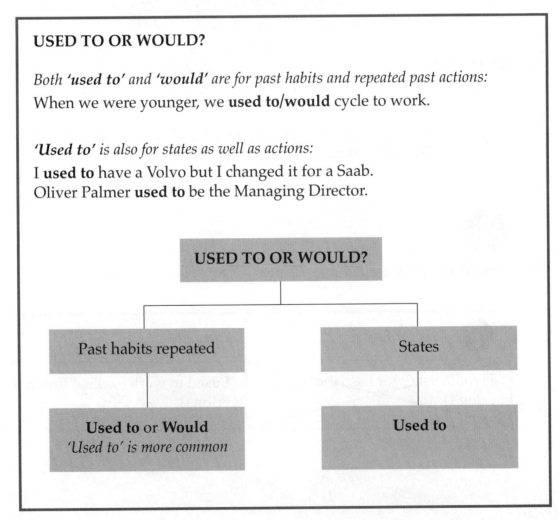

6 Present Perfect Simple (I have worked)

Situations which started in the past and continue to the present

The company **has manufactured** components for the motor industry for the last twenty years. Since 1980, they **have sold** their products through wholesalers in the United States.

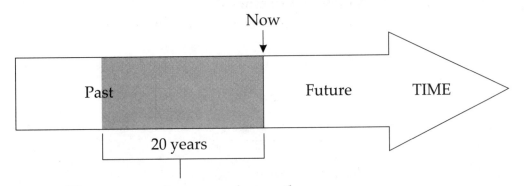

The company **has manufactured** components for the last twenty years.

Other examples

In recent years, more companies of this type **have entered** the market.
Kenneth Swan **has worked** as Product Manager for the last ten years.
We **have designed** software since 1985.
I **haven't seen** George Adams for a long time. **Have** you **had** any contact with him recently?
How long **have** you **been** in charge here?

FOR OR SINCE?

For + a period of time

He has lived in Budapest **for fifteen years**.
I've thought about this problem **for a long time**.

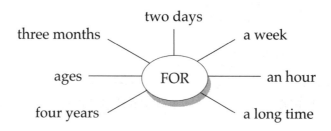

Since + a specific time in the past

He has lived in Budapest **since 1991**.
Jane's been in the office **since 8 o'clock** this morning.

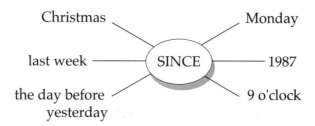

❗ Typical Error	Correct
~~I have worked for this company since four years.~~	I have worked for this company **for** four years.

Already, just, recently, yet, so far, up to now

These words and phrases are often used with the Present Perfect:

"Have you read the minutes of the meeting yet?"

"Yes. I've already passed them on to Simon."

"Good. I haven't seen him recently. Has he only just come back from his holiday?"
"Yes, he has."

There are ten candidates on the short list. I've interviewed four people so far.

We've sold about fifty books up to now.

Changed situations

> The company **has achieved** a substantial increase in profits in the last six months. It **has** also **increased** its market share by five per cent.

Other examples
Unemployment **has risen** by two per cent in the last year.
Since the end of the last financial year, the number of staff **has dropped** from six thousand to approximately five and a half thousand workers.

Situations with a present effect

> Our suppliers **have increased** their prices.
> *(This means our costs will be higher.)*

Other examples

I can't see you this week. I **have arranged** to visit our sales office in Paris.
Susan**'s** just **phoned** to say she **has missed** her train. *(She'll be late for the meeting.)*
I**'ve lost** my keys. *(I can't get into the house.)*
There **has been** an accident on the motorway. *(That's why there is a long queue of traffic.)*
I**'ve finished** the report. *(Here it is.)*

When/as soon as/after/until

> Would you come to my office **after** you **have had** your lunch, please?

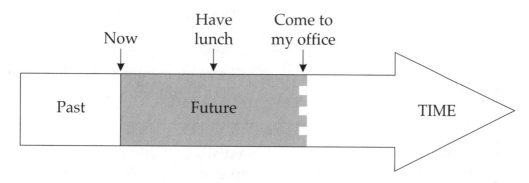

Would you come to my office **after** you
have had your lunch, please?

Other examples

I'll join you for coffee **as soon as** I **have finished** what I'm doing.
I'll talk to you again **when** I**'ve seen** Mrs. Symes about your ideas.
I'm waiting for a fax from Frankfurt. I don't want to leave the office **until** it **has arrived**.
Would you come and see me **after** you **have spoken** to him?

Note

*When the Present Perfect is used with 'when', 'as soon as', 'after' and 'until', it has a **future meaning**.*

She'll return to work **as soon as** she **has recovered** from her illness. *(She hasn't recovered yet; she will recover in the future.)*

VERBS: PRESENT, PAST AND FUTURE

Present Perfect or Past Simple?

> "Good morning, Jim. I see you've **changed** your car. When **did** you **get** this one?"
> "Yesterday. The other one **was** over five years old and I **decided** to buy a new one."

Other examples

Present Perfect	Past Simple
"**Have** you **had** a meeting with the new recruits yet?" ⇨	"Yes, I **saw** them last Wednesday." ⇩ "What **did** you **think** of them?" ⇩ "I **was** quite impressed. They **seemed** very bright and enthusiastic."
"**Have** you ever **been** to the United States?" ⇩ "Yes, I **have**. ⇨	I **went** to Maine on holiday last year." ⇩ "**Did** you **stay** in one place or **travel** around?" ⇩ "We **hired** a car and **managed** to see quite a lot. We **went** in October; the autumn colours **were** wonderful."

⚠ Typical Errors	Correct
~~I have been to London last week.~~	I **went** to London last week.
~~I have seen him yesterday.~~	I **saw** him yesterday.

Note

The **Present Perfect** always has a connection with present time and is **never** used to say **when** something happened in the past.

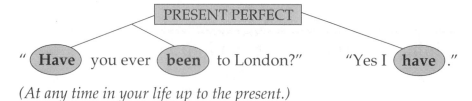

(At any time in your life up to the present.)

The **Past Simple** is used for situations that happened at a specific time in the past.

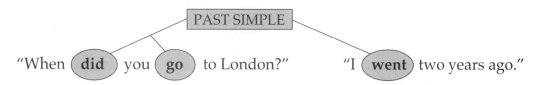

PRESENT PERFECT

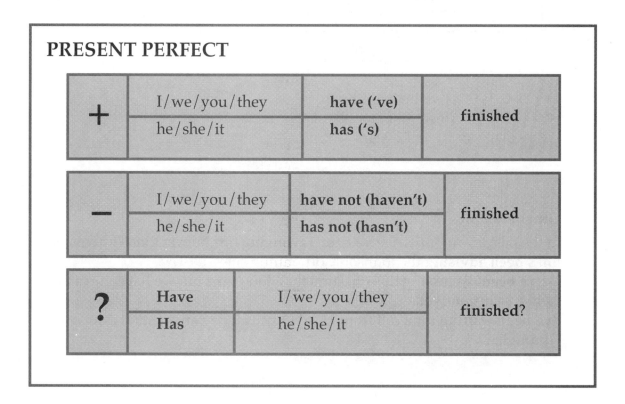

VERBS: PRESENT, PAST AND FUTURE

7 Present Perfect Continuous (I have been working)

Saying how long something has been happening

> **I've been living** in Amsterdam for about six years. At first, I worked for Elsevier, but for the past two years, **I've been working** for Unilever.

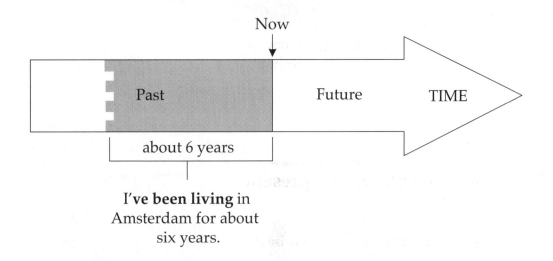

I've been living in Amsterdam for about six years.

Other examples

In the past few months, we**'ve been reviewing** our information systems.
Jim**'s been advising** the Johnson Corporation since 1991.
We**'ve been discussing** this question for a long time but we haven't reached any conclusions yet.
I**'ve been waiting** for a call from Head Office all day and it still hasn't come through.

We've been buying machine parts from your company for about seven years.

I've been trying to get through to Mr. Smith ever since I arrived in the office, but his phone is always engaged.

Helen's been doing that job for ten years.

'For' and 'Since': See *Present Perfect Simple* (Unit 6).

A continuous action which has recently stopped

> I'm sorry I'm late. My train was delayed. **Have** you **been waiting** long?

Other examples

They **have** just **been testing** the new machine. It's in good working order.

Jane and Bob are back from their holiday. They**'ve been travelling** around Italy.

Continuous actions with a present effect

> You look very tired. **Have** you **been working** too hard?

Other examples

It**'s been snowing.** *(The garden's all white.)*

"What **have** you **been doing**? Your hands are covered in oil."
"I**'ve been trying** to repair the car."

I **haven't been learning** English for long so I can't understand very much yet.

VERBS: PRESENT, PAST AND FUTURE

Present Perfect Continuous or Simple?

> "Martin **has been writing** his report for five days now. What about you?"
> "I**'ve written** mine. I finished it last night."

Contrasting examples

She**'s been learning** English for two years.
She **has learned** a lot and now she's fluent.

They**'ve been working** on a prototype for a new product but they are having some problems with it.
They**'ve finished** the prototype. It was tested last week.

PRESENT PERFECT CONTINUOUS	PRESENT PERFECT SIMPLE
We are interested in the action, not whether it has been finished or not: I**'ve been writing** the report since 10 o'clock. The company **has been developing** a new engine.	*Here the action has been finished:* I**'ve written** the report. The company **has developed** a new engine.
To say how long something has been happening: My son**'s been travelling** around Africa for six months.	*To say how many things we have completed:* He **has visited** seven countries so far.

Some verbs (Stative verbs) can only be used in the Simple, for example, 'know', 'understand', 'realise' etc.

GRAMMAR

ⓘ Typical Error	Correct
~~I have been knowing her for a very long time.~~	I **have known** her for a very long time.

PRESENT PERFECT CONTINUOUS

+	I/we/you/they	have ('ve)	been	working
	he/she/it	has ('s)		

−	I/we/you/they	have not (haven't)	been	working
	he/she/it	has not (hasn't)		

?	Have	I/we/you/they	been	working?
	Has	he/she/it		

See *Present Simple* (Unit 1) for other examples of verbs not used in the Continuous (Stative verbs).

8 Past Perfect Simple
(I had worked)

Sequence of past events

The meeting **had** already **started** when I got there just after nine o'clock.

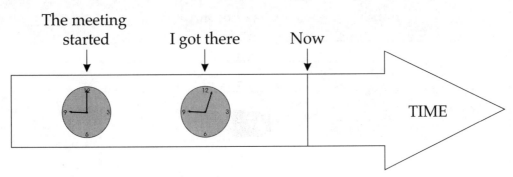

The meeting **had** already **started** when I got there.

Other examples

By the time I arrived, Michael **had left** the office.
My wife **had eaten** dinner before I got home.
Jessica apologised because she **had forgotten** to bring an important file with her.
I didn't go to the cinema with my brother last night because I **had** already **seen** the film.

They **had never been** to Berlin before so they bought a map of the city.
It was obvious that he **had not read** the report before the meeting.

Hadn't they **told** you about their plans before you went to the meeting with them?

36 GRAMMAR

PAST SIMPLE OR PAST PERFECT?

Past Simple

*When we talk about an event that happened in the past, we use the **Past Simple**.*

I **started** my present job in 1992.

I **met** Jane yesterday.

Past Perfect

*We use the **Past Perfect** to talk about something that had happened before then.*

When I started my present job in 1992, I **had** already **had** ten years' experience in sales.

I met Jane yesterday. I **hadn't seen** her for a long time as she **had been** away on holiday.

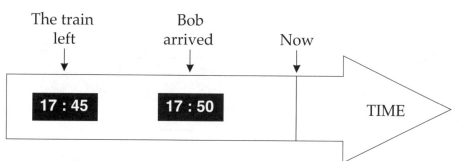

By the time Bob arrived at the station, the train **had** already **left**.

As soon as, after, until, before, when

> The Sales Director left for Paris **as soon as** he **had finished** the presentation.

Other examples

18 : 00	18 : 01
The meeting ended	I left the office

I left the office **as soon as** the meeting **had ended**.

13 : 00	13 : 30
We had lunch	Christina went out

I'm sorry Christina isn't here. She went out **after** we**'d had** lunch.

17 : 30	17 : 45
He left the factory	I phoned

David **had** already **left** the factory **when** I phoned.

Monday	Tuesday
I discussed the report with my boss	I sent out the report

I decided not to send out the report **until** I **had discussed** it with my boss.

The week before last	Last week
They made a decision about the launch date	The meeting was held

They **had** already **made** a decision about the launch date for the campaign **before** the meeting was held to discuss it with the sales team.

GRAMMAR

'Had' is sometimes shortened to 'd (I'd, he'd, she'd, we'd, you'd, they'd), especially in spoken English.

I'd forgotten all about it until you reminded me.
By the time he went to live in Dijon, **he'd** already learned to speak French.

*I'd, he'd, etc. followed by a verb in the **infinitive** means 'I would' 'he would', etc.*
I'd like some coffee, please.

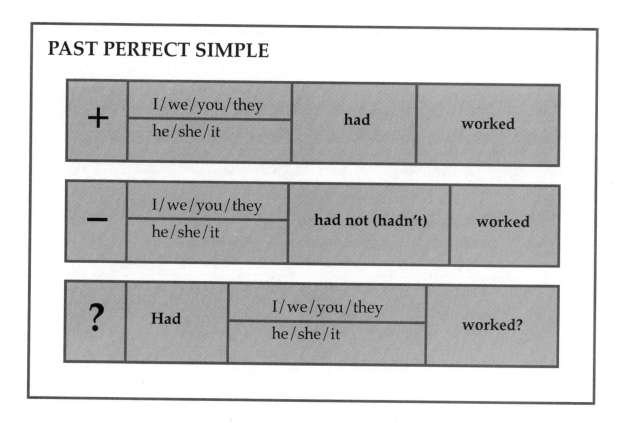

9 Past Perfect Continuous (I had been working)

Sequence of past events

We went to the airport yesterday to meet Anne and Peter but their plane **had been delayed** because of a thunderstorm. By the time it landed, we **had been waiting** for two hours.

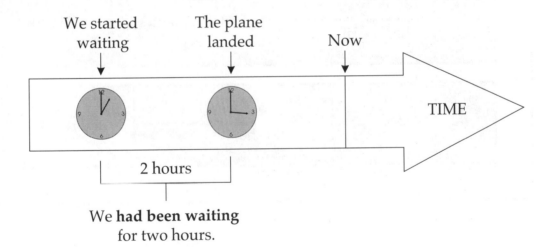

We **had been waiting** for two hours.

Other examples

Tom **had been working** for the company for over twenty years when he was made redundant.

We **had been living** in London since 1970 so we decided to buy a house in the country when we retired.

Before I came to live in England, I **had been learning** English for about three years.

Note

*We use the **Past Perfect Continuous** when we wish to emphasize **how long** something had been happening before another event happened:*

I **had been driving** for three hours when the accident happened.

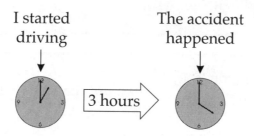

*We also use the **Continuous** for an action which takes some time (and is not completed quickly):*

The river flooded because it **had been raining** for three days.

It is important to remember that some verbs (Stative verbs) are not used in Continuous tenses (e.g. belong, know).

❗ Typical Error	Correct
~~I had been belonging to the tennis club for ten years when they built a new clubhouse.~~	I **had belonged** to the tennis club for ten years when they built a new clubhouse.

See *Present Simple* (Unit 1) for examples of other verbs not used in the Continuous.

PAST PERFECT CONTINUOUS

+	I/we/you/they he/she/it	had	been	working
−	I/we/you/they he/she/it	had not (hadn't)	been	working

?	Had	I/we/you/they he/she/it	been	working?

10 Going to

Intentions and plans

> In order to attract new customers, we're going to widen our product range.

Other examples

I'm going to telephone him as soon as I have more details.
We're going to hold a planning meeting on Friday next week.
The company is going to open a new branch in Scandinavia.

I'm not going to order the new computer until after my holiday.

What are you going to do about the problem?
Are they going to invest in Samuelsons?

Predicting future events from present evidence

> Hanson plc have shown a great deal of interest in the company. I think they're going to make a takeover bid.

Other examples

It's very humid today. I think it's going to thunder.
Economic conditions are getting worse. It's going to be a difficult year for the company.

Pierre has just phoned from Paris. He's missed his flight, so he**'s not going to** be here until late afternoon.

Do you think that the Deutschmark **is going to** weaken against the dollar?

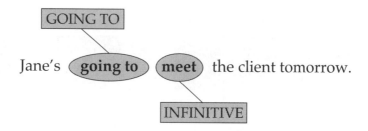

GOING TO

+	I	am ('m)	going to	work
	he/she/it	is ('s)		
	we/you/they	are ('re)		

−	I	am not ('m not)	going to	work
	he/she/it	is not (isn't)		
	we/you/they	are not (aren't)		

?	Am	I	going to	work?
	Is	he/she/it		
	Are	we/you/they		

See also *Present Simple* (Unit 1), *Present Continuous* (Unit 2), and *Will* (Unit 11).

TALKING ABOUT FUTURE TIME

There are several ways of referring to future time in English. These are the most common forms:

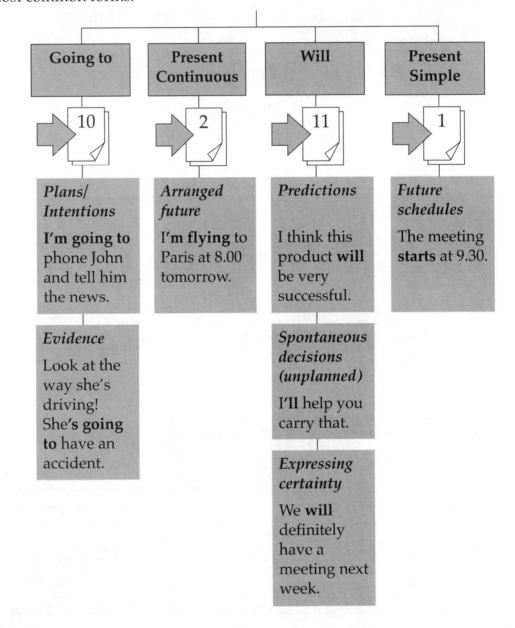

Typical Errors	Correct
~~What will you do tonight?~~	What **are** you **going to do** tonight? / What **are** you **doing** tonight?
~~I will play tennis with my brother on Saturday.~~	**I'm going to play** tennis with my brother on Saturday. / **I'm playing** tennis with my brother on Saturday.

11 Will

Predicting future events

> "What time do you expect our French visitors to arrive?"
> "I think they'**ll** be here by about twelve. We'**ll** have lunch as soon as they arrive."

Other examples

The Marketing Manager thinks the new brochure **will** be ready by the end of the year.

"Do you think Patrick's idea **will** work?"
"I hope it **will**. I expect he'**ll** give us more information about it at next week's meeting."

If current trends continue, I think there'**ll** be a fall in interest rates.
I expect that James Beal **will** sell his shares in the company if he can find a buyer.
He'**ll** lose his job if he's not careful.
The report **won't** be finished until the end of next week.

Think, hope and expect

Will is often used after '**think**', '**hope**', and '**expect**' when predicting future events:

Harry **hopes** the Board **will** agree to his proposal.
I **don't think** it **will** rain tomorrow.
We **expect** that the the Chairman **will** want to call a meeting within the next few weeks.

Spontaneous (unplanned) decisions

(On the telephone)
"Hi, Mike. It's Joanna. Is your report ready yet?"
"Yes. I'**ll** send you a copy, but remember it's confidential."
"Fine. I **won't** show it to the others."

Other examples

I **won't** finish this job tonight. It's too late now. I'**ll** finish it tomorrow.

"I've got to leave now, but I haven't spoken to Mary yet about the changes we're planning."
"Don't worry. I'**ll** talk to her this afternoon."
"Thanks."

"It's terribly hot in here."
"I'**ll** open the window."

"Which of you wants to give the presentation?"
"I'**ll** do it."

Note

'**Will**' is **not** used for planned or arranged actions. (We use 'Going to' or the Present Continuous.)

❗ Typical Error	Correct
I can't have lunch with you tomorrow because I will go to the planning meeting.	I can't have lunch with you tomorrow because I'**m going to** the planning meeting.

For future arrangements and plans, see Present Continuous (Unit 2) and Going to (Unit 10).

VERBS: PRESENT, PAST AND FUTURE

Expressing degrees of certainty

You **will** certainly be the first person to be told when we receive the information.

Other examples

We're going to Scotland this weekend. We'**ll** probably go by car but we haven't decided yet.
There **will** possibly be some redundancies in the company if the recession continues.
We certainly **won't** be taking on any new staff until next year.
Philippe Lacroix **will** almost certainly be the next Chairman of the company.

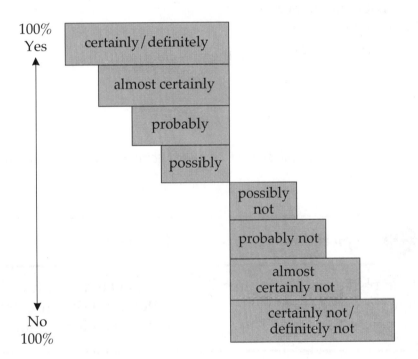

See also Modal Verbs *Will and Would* (Unit 21).

GRAMMAR

WILL

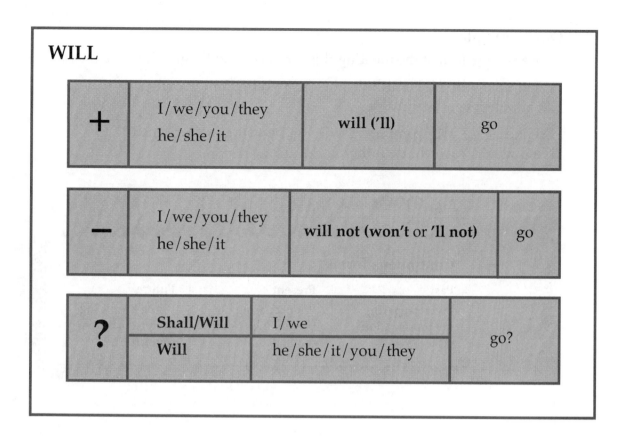

Will be ...ing (Future Continuous)

I'm going on holiday. This time next week, **I'll be swimming** in the Indian Ocean.

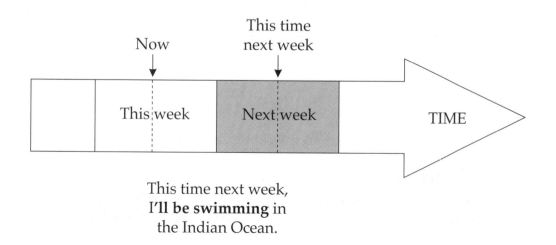

This time next week, **I'll be swimming** in the Indian Ocean.

Other examples

I'll be seeing Tom at the meeting this afternoon, so I'll give him the message.

"What time **will** the Finnish visitors **be arriving** tomorrow?"
"At about eleven, I think."

"I'd like to use your computer. **Will** you **be using** it after lunch?"
"No, I won't. You can use it then."

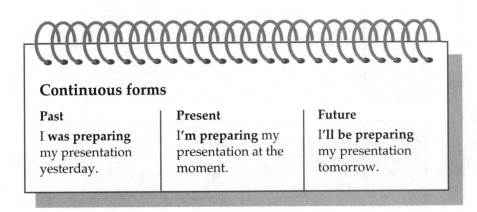

Will have done (Future Perfect)

I'll have finished my report by Thursday.

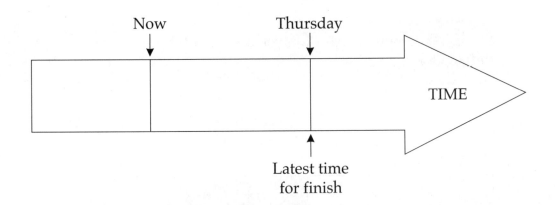

I'll have finished my report by Thursday.

Other examples

Next year, my wife and I **will have been married** for twenty-five years.
Come to the office at two o'clock. We**'ll have finished** lunch by then.

Perfect forms

Past	Present	Future
David **had worked** for the company for fifteen years when he was promoted to the board five years ago.	David **has worked** for this company for twenty years.	In five years time, David **will have worked** for this company for twenty-five years.

FUTURE CONTINUOUS	FUTURE PERFECT
Talking about plans: "What **will** you **be doing** tomorrow afternoon?" "**I'll be playing** golf."	*Saying that something will be completed by a certain time in the future:* "Next year, **I'll have been** an engineer for ten years."

FUTURE CONTINUOUS

+	I	will ('ll)	be	working	tomorrow

FUTURE PERFECT

+	I	will ('ll)	have	finished	by tomorrow

VERBS: PRESENT, PAST AND FUTURE

TALKING ABOUT FUTURE TIME

There are several ways of referring to future time in English. These are the most common forms:

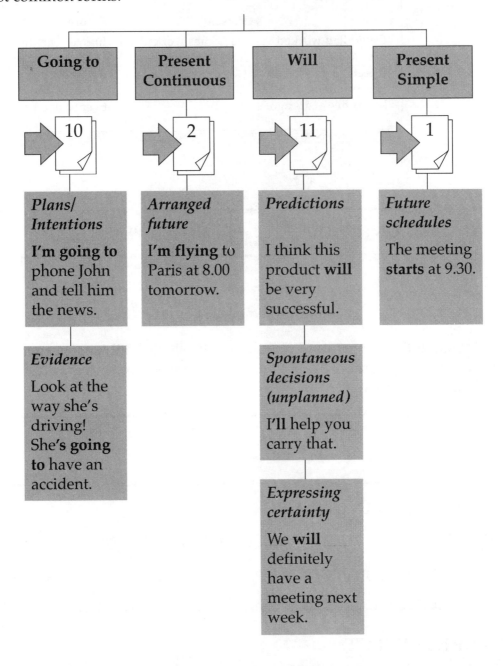

⚠ Typical Error	Correct
I can't meet you on Saturday because I will play tennis with my daughter.	I can't meet you on Saturday because **I'm playing** tennis with my daughter.

GRAMMAR

12 Passive

Use of the Passive

The house **was built** in 1980.

Other examples

Active	Passive
James Austin **established** the company ten years ago.	The company **was established** ten years ago by James Austin.
Someone **has stolen** my car.	My car **has been stolen**.
They **have** just **opened** the new warehouse.	The new warehouse **has** just **been opened**.

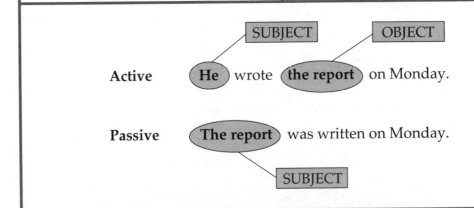

Active: He wrote the report on Monday. (SUBJECT / OBJECT)

Passive: The report was written on Monday. (SUBJECT)

Note

We normally use the passive when we are not interested in or do not know who carried out the action.

The letter **was posted** yesterday morning.
She **was injured** in a road accident.

In English, the Past Simple in the passive is used to say when or where someone was born.

❗ Typical Errors	Correct
~~Janet is born in 1970.~~	Janet **was born** in 1970.
~~My brother and I are born in London.~~	My brother and I **were born** in London.

Have something done (Causative)

We use '**have something done**' when someone else does something for us.

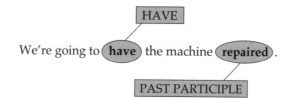

I'll be a bit late tomorrow. I've got to take the car to the garage. **I'm having** it **serviced**.

When **did** you **have** your hair **cut**?

We **have** the 'Financial Times' **delivered** to our house every morning.

We **have had** air conditioning installed in the offices.

Jill**'s having** a new house **built** in the country.

VERBS: PASSIVE

Passive forms

> When the products leave the factory, they **are packaged** and stored in the warehouse. When they **are needed**, they **are taken** out of the warehouse. They **are** then **loaded** on to the delivery van and **distributed** to customers.

Other examples

Present Simple
In some restaurants, service **is included** in the price.

Present Continuous
Your invoice **is being prepared** at the moment.

Past Simple
Taxes **were raised** in April.

Past Continuous
The building **was being renovated** when I was there.

Present Perfect
A new Financial Director **has** just **been appointed**.

Past Perfect
The commission **had been increased** before the new agents were appointed.

Infinitive
Cigarettes must **be extinguished** when we enter the factory.

Perfect Infinitive
The parcel might **have been damaged** in transit.

Note

The Passive form = 'be' followed by the Past Participle of the main verb:

Over fifty people are employed in the Leipzig plant.

PASSIVE FORMS

	Subject	+ 'be' (in correct tense)	+ past participle of verb
Present Simple	It It	is is	made. cleaned.
Present Continuous	It It	is being is being	made. cleaned.
Past Simple	It It	was was	made. cleaned.
Past Continuous	It It	was being was being	made. cleaned.
Present Perfect	It It	has been has been	made. cleaned.
Past Perfect	It It	had been had been	made. cleaned.
Infinitive	It should It should	be be	made. cleaned.
Perfect Infinitive	It should It should	have been have been	made. cleaned.

For *past participles* see list of *Irregular Verbs* (Unit 96).

13 Conditionals (if...): Introduction

Position of 'if'

> **If** we start work on the new brochure in January, it will be ready for publication by the end of March.
>
> or
>
> The new brochure will be ready for publication by the end of March **if** we start work on it in January.

Other examples

If we increase production, we should be able to meet the demand.
We should be able to meet the demand **if** we increase production.

If we hadn't delivered the order on time, we would have lost the customer.
We would have lost the customer **if** we hadn't delivered the order on time.

Note

'If' can be at the beginning of the sentence, or in the middle (at the beginning of the second clause).

If	prices rise,	the volume of sales usually falls.	
The volume of sales usually falls		if	prices rise.

(Note the **comma** which is necessary in the first example.)

Providing (that), provided (that), as long as

These phrases have the same meaning as **'if'**, but **'providing/provided that'** are a little more formal.

We are prepared to offer a ten per cent discount **providing (that)** you order over one thousand items.

I can give you a lift to the station **as long as** you are ready by five o'clock.

He's taking the children to the beach tomorrow **provided (that)** the weather is good.

Unless

'Unless' = if not

We won't be able to compete **if** we **don't** increase productivity.

or

We won't be able to compete **unless** we increase productivity.

'Unless' is often used to give a warning:

We'll make a loss this year **unless** sales pick up in the final quarter.

'When' or 'if'?

"I'll show this sales report to Alan Johnson **when** I see him tomorrow."
"Could you ask Simon to look at it as well?"
"I don't know whether Simon is coming to the meeting. **If** he does, I'll give him a copy."

Other examples

Please switch off the computer **when** you leave.
Staff should switch off their computers **if** they leave the office for more than one hour.

I'll phone him **when** I get home.
I'll phone him from the office **if** I get there before five o'clock.

If the trial of the prototype is successful, we'll go ahead with the project.
When the trial is finished, we'll start full production.

Note

'When' and *'if'* are not the same.
'When' is used when something is certain to happen.
'If' is used when it is uncertain whether something will happen or not.

WHEN (Certain)	IF (Uncertain)
I'll give it to him **when** I see him. (I am **definitely** going to see him).	I'll give it to him **if** I see him. (It is **uncertain** whether I will see him or not).

❗ Typical Error	Correct
~~I think he'll probably get the job. I'll be surprised when he doesn't.~~	I think he'll probably get the job. I'll be surprised **if** he doesn't.

See also *When or If* (Unit 46).

14 Conditional 0

General truths, laws, rules, and warnings

If you **are** a citizen of the UK, you **can work** in any other country in the European Union.

CONDITION
If you **are** a citizen of the UK,

RESULT
you **can work** in any other EU country.

Other examples

If you **start up** a new company, you **must register** it with the authorities.
If the temperature gauge **is** on red, the engine **is** too hot.
If the red light **goes** on, **switch** the machine off.
If someone **lives** in France for more than 183 days in a year, he **has to pay** tax there.

I **can't understand** you **if** you **speak** too quickly.
You **must work** hard **if** you **want to** succeed.
He **might agree** to do it **if** we **ask** him.

CONDITIONAL 0

IF + PRESENT + PRESENT

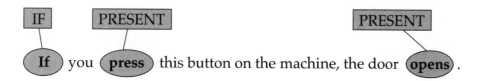

If you press this button on the machine, the door opens.

IF + PRESENT + MODAL VERB

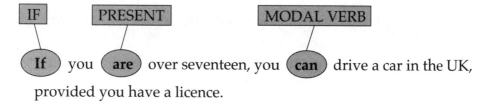

If you are over seventeen, you can drive a car in the UK, provided you have a licence.

IF + PRESENT + IMPERATIVE

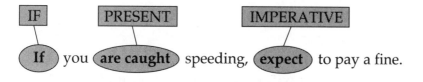

If you are caught speeding, expect to pay a fine.

15 Conditional 1

Real possibilities

> If we **restructure** the company, it **will result** in a lot of redundancies.

CONDITION
If we **restructure** the company,

RESULT
it **will result** in a lot of redundancies.

Other examples

If they **don't improve** their quality of service, they**'ll lose** a lot of customers.
If there **is** a rise in demand, we**'ll try** to meet it with our existing resources.
If the recession **continues,** many more companies **will go** out of business.
If you **are** free tomorrow, we **can** continue our discussion then.
You**'ll regret** it if you **don't accept** their offer.
Unless you **leave** now, you **won't be** in time for the start of the conference.

We use this conditional (Conditional 1) when we feel that there is a real possibility that something will happen:

If we **miss** the nine o'clock train, we**'ll** have to catch the 9.40.
(The speaker thinks there is a real possibility that they will miss the nine o'clock train.)

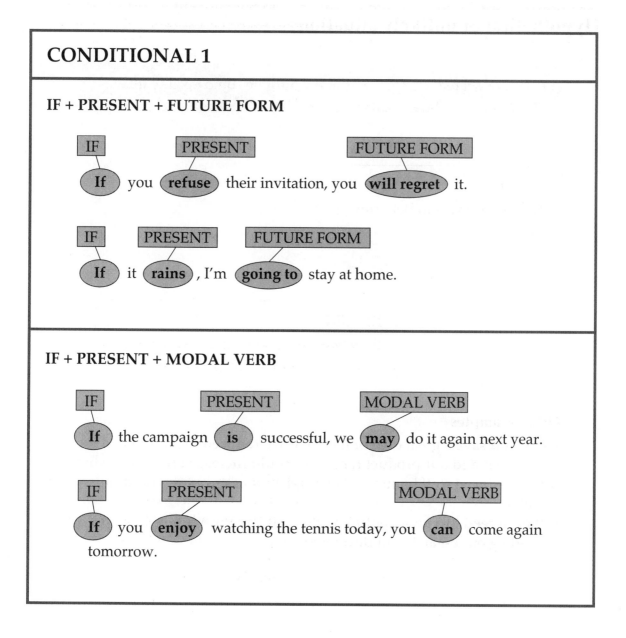

16 Conditional 2

Hypothetical or unlikely situations

If you **relocated** to Belgium, there **would** be some tax advantages.

CONDITION
If you **relocated** to Belgium,

RESULT
there **would be** some tax advantages.

Other examples

We **would save** a great deal of money **if** we **reduced** the number of workers.
If we **expanded** our product range, we **could increase** our market share.
If they **reduced** staff bonuses, they **might cut** costs but it **would cause** a lot of trouble.
If they **agreed** to a joint venture with our company, we **would** all **reduce** our spending on research and development.

CONDITIONAL 2 OR 1?

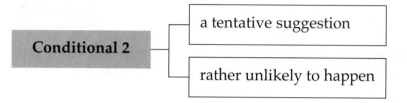

If you **opened** a branch in Sweden, you **would be able** to sell into Finland and Norway too.

(The company may not have discussed this possibility seriously yet. The meaning is "Let's consider what would happen if...")

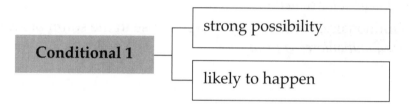

If you **open** a branch in Sweden, you **will be able** to sell into Finland and Norway too.

(There is already a strong possibility that a branch will be opened in Sweden.)

❗ Typical Error	Correct
If he ~~would practise~~ more, he would be ~~the~~ best player in ~~the~~ world.	If he **practised** more, he would be the best player in the world.

VERBS: CONDITIONALS

Unreal states and situations

> If I **were** rich, I **would retire** immediately.

Other examples

If you **didn't smoke** so much, you**'d be** much healthier.
If I **weren't** so busy, I**'d be** glad to help.
(But I am busy so I can't.)
If I **had** his telephone number with me, I**'d phone** him.
(But I haven't got his number.)
If he **practised** more, he**'d be** one of the best tennis players in the world.

Conditional 2 is used for something 'unreal':
If I **were** a millionaire, I **would buy** a large house in the south of France.
(But I am not a millionaire, so I can't.)

Giving advice

> If I **were** you, I**'d drive** to London, rather than take the train.

Other examples

If I **were** you, I **would concentrate** the marketing campaign on the Paris area.
If I **were** you, I**'d start** the presentation by talking about last month's sales performance.
If I **were** you, I**'d see** a doctor about your headaches.

Note

'I were' is often used when giving advice, *"If I were you..."*
If I **were you,** I'd stop smoking.

CONDITIONAL 2

IF + PAST + COULD + INFINITIVE

IF + PAST + MIGHT + INFINITIVE

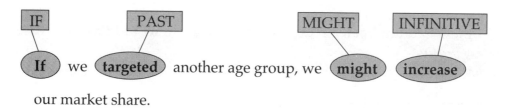

our market share.

IF + WERE + WOULD + INFINITIVE

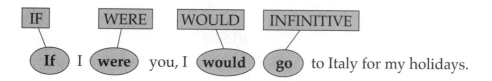

IF + PAST + WOULD + INFINITIVE

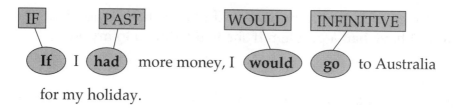

for my holiday.

17 Conditional 3

Speculating about past events

If there **had not been** a recession in Europe, we **would have increased** our profits.

CONDITION
If there **had not been** a recession in Europe

RESULT
we **would have increased** our profits.

Other examples

If I **had known** you were coming, I **could have met** you at the airport.
If I **had thought** about it more carefully, I **would** probably **have reached** a different decision.
If he **had driven** more carefully, he **wouldn't have had** an accident.
She **wouldn't have had** a problem **if** she **had listened** to my advice.

Note

Conditional 3 is often used to express regret about something that happened or did not happen in the past:

If we **had submitted** a lower estimate, we **would have been chosen** for the work. (*But we didn't do this, we submitted a higher estimate.*)

We can also say:
I wish we had submitted a lower estimate.

CONDITIONAL 3

IF + PAST PERFECT + COULD HAVE + PAST PARTICIPLE

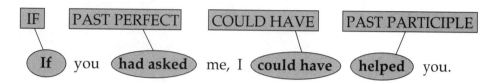

If you had asked me, I could have helped you.

IF + PAST PERFECT + WOULD HAVE + PAST PARTICIPLE

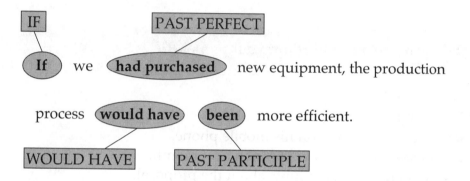

If we had purchased new equipment, the production process would have been more efficient.

IF + PAST PERFECT + MIGHT HAVE + PAST PARTICIPLE

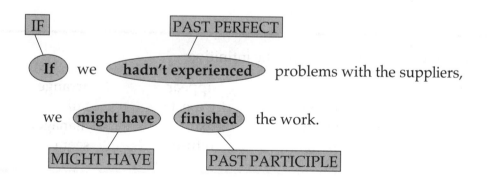

If we hadn't experienced problems with the suppliers, we might have finished the work.

18 Infinitive ([To] work)

Infinitive after certain verbs

> Did the Board **agree to adopt** your proposal?

Other examples
I **managed to reach** him on his mobile phone.
I **hope to see** you when I visit Milan next month.
You **seem to have** some doubts about the proposal.
We have **decided** not **to enter** the Chinese market.
We can't **afford to invest** any more money at the moment.
We **expect to recover** our investment within four years.
They have **arranged to hold** the next sales conference in Rome.

These verbs are followed by the infinitive:

afford	agree	appear	arrange
attempt	decide	expect	fail
hope	intend	learn	manage
mean	plan	refuse	seem

Some verbs can be followed by either the infinitive or the gerund. See page 75.

74 GRAMMAR

INFINITIVE (TO WORK) OR GERUND (WORKING)?

Begin and start

These verbs can be followed by:

Infinitive	or	Gerund
I started **to work** on the project four years ago.		I started **working** on the project four years ago.

Like, hate, regret, remember and stop

These verbs are sometimes followed by the infinitive and sometimes by the gerund (**...ing**), but the meaning is different:

Infinitive	Gerund
I like **to go** to the dentist every six months. *I think it is sensible to do this.*	I like **going** for walks in the countryside. *I enjoy this.*
We regret **to inform** you that the meeting has been cancelled. *We are sorry to tell you that the meeting has been cancelled.*	I regret **making** that mistake. *I made the mistake in the past and wish I hadn't.*
I remembered **to post** the letter yesterday. *I did not forget to do it.*	I remember **posting** the letter yesterday. *I did it and I remember the action.*
Jim stopped **to smoke** a cigarette. *He stopped what he was doing in order to smoke a cigarette.*	Jane stopped **smoking** two years ago. *She gave up smoking and she no longer smokes.*

Verb + noun/pronoun + infinitive

> George asked me **to write** a reference for him when he left the company.

Other examples

The injection of capital from the parent company enabled us **to launch** several new projects.

He persuaded me **to try** hang gliding.

We don't allow anyone **to smoke** in the laboratory.

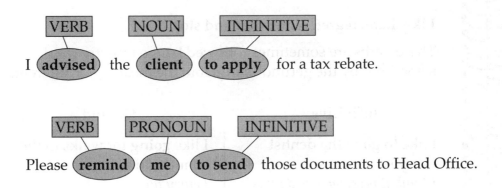

Advise and recommend

You advise someone **'to do'** something:
We strongly **advise you to review** your control procedures.

'Recommend' is followed by **'that'**, *not* **'to'**.

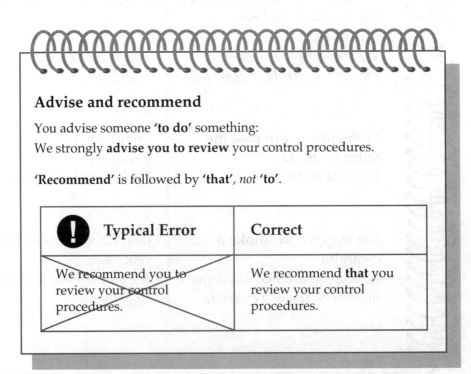

Want, ask, and expect

'**Want**', '**ask**', and '**expect**' are sometimes used with an *object (a noun or pronoun)* and sometimes without:

Jack **wants** *me* **to phone** him tomorrow.
Angela **wants to move** to the London office.

Michael **asked** *me* **to find out** how long it would take them to deliver the new printer.
(On the telephone)
I **asked to speak** to the Accounts Office but I was cut off.

A manager **expects** *his staff* **to work** efficiently.
I **expect to arrive** in Berlin at 11 o'clock.

To be + ...ing (continuous actions)

> I didn't want to be disturbed so I pretended **to be reading** something important.

Other examples

I wanted to speak to Martin but he appears **to be talking** to some visitors.
I had a postcard from Philip and Anne. They seem **to be enjoying** their holiday.

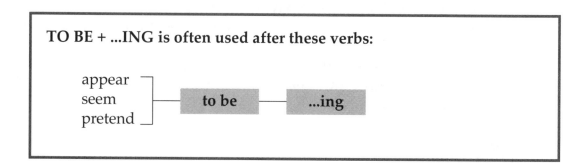

TO BE + ...ING is often used after these verbs:

appear
seem
pretend
→ to be → ...ing

VERBS: INFINITIVE AND GERUND

To have + past participle (completed actions)

> I seem **to have lost** the address you gave me.

Other examples
I wanted to talk to him but he appears **to have gone** home.
He seems **to have mislaid** his wallet.

TO HAVE + PAST PARTICIPLE is often used after these verbs:

appear, seem — to have — past participle

Make and let

> The director **let** her secretary **leave** work early on Friday.

Other examples
I was so tired yesterday, I had to **make** myself **concentrate**.
We'll have to try and **make** them **pay** on time.
The training session was very interesting. It **made** us **think** about reviewing our appraisal system.
I don't **let** my son **stay** out after 11 o'clock, he's still too young.
We'll **let** the new recruits **introduce** themselves before we start the induction course.

In the passive, 'make' is followed by the infinitive with 'to':
I only agreed to that decision because I **was made to do** so.

'Make' or 'let' + pronoun or noun + infinitive without 'to':

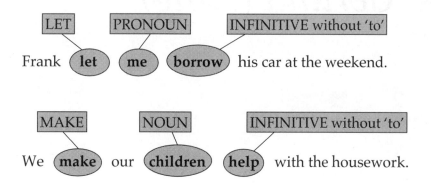

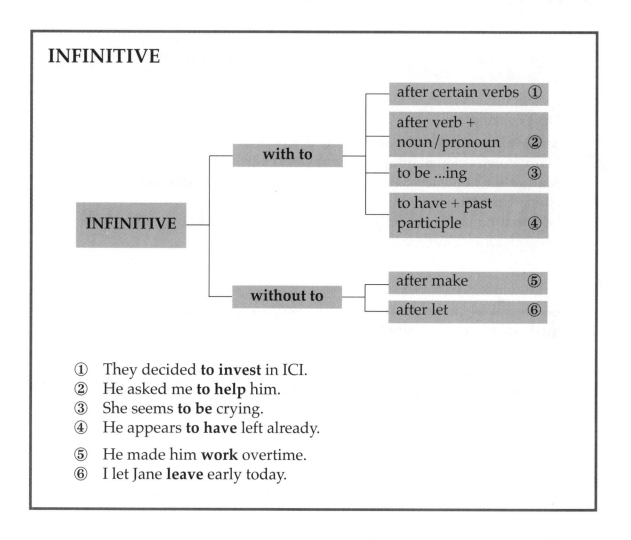

① They decided **to invest** in ICI.
② He asked me **to help** him.
③ She seems **to be** crying.
④ He appears **to have** left already.

⑤ He made him **work** overtime.
⑥ I let Jane **leave** early today.

See also *Gerund* (Unit 19).

VERBS: INFINITIVE AND GERUND

19 Gerund (...ing)

Gerund as the subject or object of a sentence

> **Increasing** the market share must be our main priority this season.

Other examples
Smoking is banned in many public places now.
I very much enjoy **playing** tennis at weekends.
Maintaining contact with customers is an important function of this department.
Negotiating internationally can be difficult without knowledge of other negotiators' cultural backgrounds.

Gerund after certain verbs

> I can't recall **giving** him the report to read.

Other examples
James suggested **meeting** the Purchasing Manager from Volkswagen.
We have postponed **printing** the new brochure until next month.
Have you considered **opening** a new branch in Singapore?
She's finished **writing** the report at last!

Some verbs can be followed by either the gerund or the infinitive, for example, 'like' see page 75.

These verbs are followed by the gerund:

avoid	commence	consider	delay
dislike	enjoy	finish	imagine
mention	miss	postpone	practise
recall	risk	suggest	

Gerund after prepositions

He avoided giving an answer to the question **by asking** one himself.

Other examples

If I were you, I'd give **up smoking**.
He left **without leaving** his contact number in Paris.
The company made substantial profits in spite **of having** a bad start to the year.
I've been in England for two years now so I am used **to driving** on the left.

When a verb *immediately* follows a preposition, it *always* ends in '...ing' (the gerund).

❗ Typical Errors	Correct
I look forward to see you soon.	I look forward to **seeing** you soon.
After to finish the report, he went home.	After **finishing** the report, he went home.
I am used to speak French. I do it every day.	I am used to **speaking** French. I do it every day.

VERBS: INFINITIVE AND GERUND

After 'mind'

> Would you mind **helping** me with these calculations?

Other examples

Would you mind **opening** the window? It's very warm in here.
Would you mind not **smoking** in here, please?
Would you mind **giving** these papers to the Sales Manager?
I don't mind **waiting** till you come back.
David said that he wouldn't mind **working** late this evening.

'Would you mind ...ing...?' is used when you ask another person to do something for you:
Would you mind posting these letters for me?

When you ask if you can do something, you use 'Do you mind if I...?':
Do you mind if I smoke?

Completed actions (having...)

> They regretted **having** lost the contract.

Other examples

They admitted **having** made several mistakes in the bill.
He denied **having** received the letter.
They closed the meeting, **having** agreed to implement the changes.
She finished the book, **having** enjoyed it a lot.

Gerund and Present Participle ('...ing')

Sometimes, the '**...ing**' form is called the Gerund but when it is part of a continuous tense, it is called the Present Participle.

Gerund	**Present Participle**
Working on this project is very interesting.	Janet is **working** on a new project this month.
Learning how to use a new computer package can take a long time.	He is **learning** how to use the new computer package.

See also *Infinitive* (Unit 18).

20 Modal Verbs: Introduction

What are modal verbs?

> We'll start the marketing campaign in June. We **may** need to call in the design team for a meeting next week as we **must** get down to planning the new brochure.

Other examples

Could I borrow your pen for a moment?
We **may** decide to open a subsidiary in Finland.
We **mustn't** forget to pay the suppliers at the end of this month.
I'll phone you tomorrow morning.
He isn't in the office at the moment. He **should** be here tomorrow.

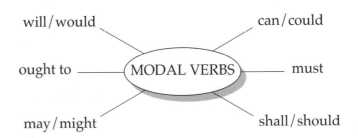

Note

The form of a modal verb is always the same:

I/you/he/she/it/we/they **can** swim.

He can*s*
She must*s*
It will*s*

Modal verb + infinitive of another verb

> I **must leave** now for the airport. My plane goes at eleven. **Can** you **call** me at the Stockholm office tomorrow?

Other examples
He **might be** late.
Would you **like** a cup of coffee?
Can you **speak** to Jane about this?

Note
Most modal verbs are followed by the infinitive of another verb, without 'to'.

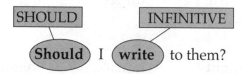

'Ought' is followed by the infinitive with 'to'.

❗ Typical Errors	Correct
I ~~must to~~ hurry. I will be late.	I **must** hurry. I will be late.
I ~~must to write him~~ a letter.	I **must** write him a letter.
I ~~can to~~ speak English.	I **can** speak English.

MODAL VERBS

Modal verbs and word order

	①	②	
John	can't	come	to the meeting next week.

① = modal verb   ② = other verb

Other examples

	①	②	
Will	you	come	to dinner on Saturday?
You	mustn't	forget	to post the letter. It's important.
It	might	rain	tomorrow.
This report	must	be finished	by Friday.

A modal verb is always the first verb in a sentence.

Questions and negatives with modal verbs

Will you give this to Charles, please? **Can** you tell him it's from me?

Other examples
Can I read last month's sales report?
Must you leave so early?

You **shouldn't** sit in the sun for too long. You'll get burnt.
I **can't** understand this table of figures. **Can** you explain it to me, please?
Where **should** I put this?

'Do', 'does', 'don't' and *'doesn't'* (and other auxiliary verbs, for example, *'did'* and *'didn't'*) are not used with modal verbs for questions and negatives.

❗ Typical Errors	Correct
~~Do you must go so soon?~~	**Must** you go so soon?
~~Do you can speak Russian?~~	**Can** you speak Russian?
~~I don't can understand this.~~	I **can't** understand this.

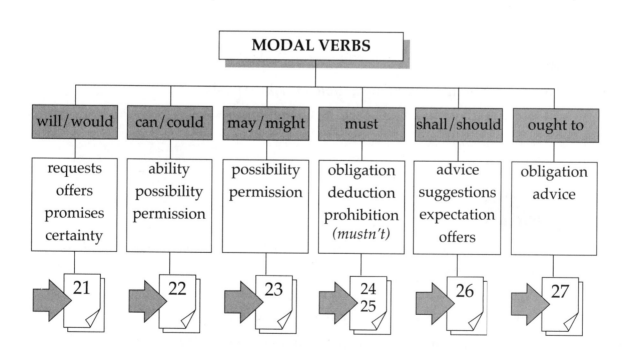

MODAL VERBS

87

21 Will and Would

Requests (will/would)

> (On the telephone)
> "I'm sorry, Elizabeth Sykes isn't in the office at the moment."
> "**Would** you ask her to call me at home, please?"

Other examples
Would you shut the door, please?
Would you pass me that book, please?
Will you let me know whether you can get to the meeting next Tuesday?
Here's the draft contract. **Will** you tell me what you think about it?

Note
Requests
'Will' and *'would'* are used with *'you'* to make requests:
Would you give this to the Accounts Clerk, please?

'Would' is more polite and formal than *'will'*, and is often followed by *'please'*.
Would you open the door, please?

'Will' is often used when talking to colleagues or friends:
Will you give this to Marion when you see her?

'Will' can be used as a command from a boss to an employee.
Will you do this today?

Offers and promises (I'll /shall I...?)

> (A colleague is carrying a lot of files)
> Wait a minute! **I'll** help you with those.

Other examples
I'll phone you tomorrow.
I'll give you a lift to the airport on Friday if you like.
I'll fax the figures through to you so you can look at them before we meet.
We'll meet you at the restaurant at seven o'clock this evening.
Shall I help you with that?

Note
'Shall', is used in the question with 'I' and 'we' to make offers:
Shall we help you with those estimates?

Expressing degrees of certainty (will)

> The management training programme **will** definitely begin in April.

Other examples
Using the new equipment **will** certainly increase running costs.
Petrol prices **will** rise in the new year.
We **will** probably not issue a new brochure until next January.

For predictions and other future uses of *Will,* see (Unit 11).
See also *Degrees of Certainty*, page 50.

MODAL VERBS

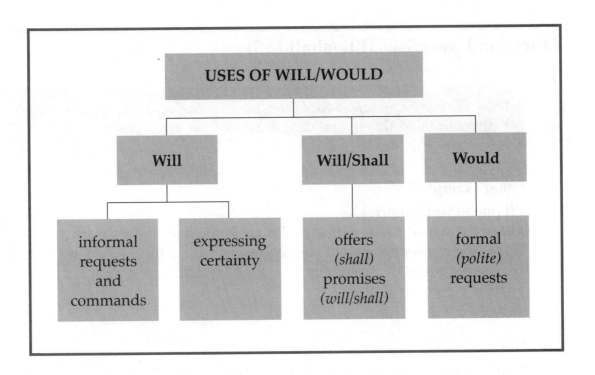

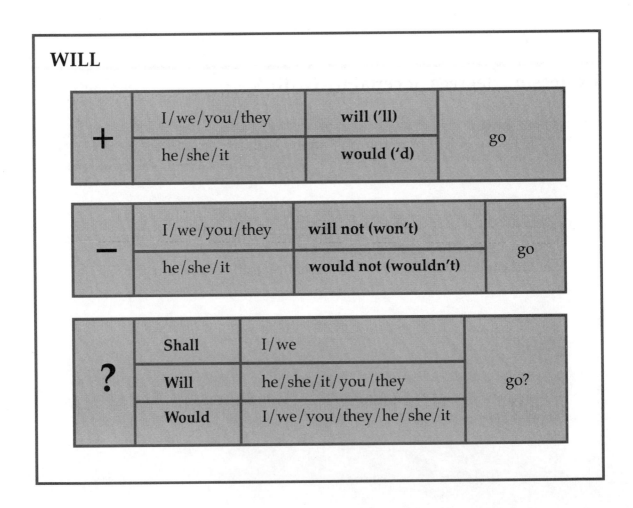

22 Can and Could

Ability

> We **can** decide how to structure the training programme at this meeting, but we **can't** decide on the location until next week.

Present ability
The new copier **can** collate and staple copies together.
Would you translate this for me, please? I **can't** understand it.
I **can't** reach the files on the top shelf. Would you help me, please?
Can you speak much Italian now you've been in Italy for a year?

Future ability
I'm afraid Mr. Stroud is busy today but he **can** see you tomorrow.
We **can** take on some extra staff next year.
The Managing Director **can't** come to the meeting next week.

Past ability
When I was younger, I **could** play the piano quite well.
He **couldn't** speak English before he joined the international sales team.
I tried to buy a mobile phone yesterday but I **couldn't** find one that I liked.
Could your children swim before they started school?

Able to: present, future and past ability

1. **'Able to'** is sometimes used for **present ability** (but it is not very common).
   Are you **able to** translate this for me?

2. **'Able to'** is also used for **future ability**:
   I think we**'ll be able to** work out a solution to the problem tomorrow.

3. **'Able to'** is used for **past ability** (when someone did or did not manage to do something that was potentially difficult):
   He was transferred to London two months ago. He **was able to** find a house quickly.
   (Finding a house in London is often difficult.)

'Able to' is followed by the infinitive:

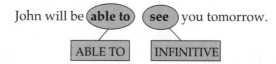

John will be **able to** **see** you tomorrow.
ABLE TO   INFINITIVE

Possibility: can/can't/could

Don't worry about it. Anyone **can** make a mistake like that.

Other examples

These machines **can** sometimes break down.
I travel a lot for my work. It **can** be very tiring.
There's a call for you from the States. It **could** be the person you met last week in New York.

"I'm not sure whether the Sales Director is in Turin or Milan today."
"He **can't** be in Turin. He had his meeting in Turin three days ago."

Note

'Can' indicates a stronger possibility than 'could'.
I can phone you tomorrow. (*There is no problem phoning.*)
I could phone you tomorrow. (*There might be a problem phoning.*)

MODAL VERBS

Permission

> "Mr. Goodall, **can** I take my holiday at the end of July this year?"
> "Yes, that should be all right."

Other examples

I'm afraid I haven't got the information with me. **Can** I phone you tomorrow?
Could I disturb you for a moment, please?
You **can** borrow my car to take your visitor to the station.

"**Could** I look into it tomorrow? I've got a lot of other things to do today."
"No, I'm sorry you **can't**. It must be done today."

Note

We use 'could' or 'can' to ask for permission. 'Could' is more formal than 'can'.

Can't have/could have/couldn't have

> You **can't have** finished that job already! You only started it half an hour ago.

Other examples

I tried to phone the sales office but there's no one there. The meeting **can't have** finished yet.
That **can't have** been Mr. Fraser that you saw. He's away on holiday.

That **could have** been the reason for the problem.
We'll have to start the meeting without James. I don't know why he's late. I suppose he **could have** missed his train.

The letter **couldn't have** arrived yet. It was only posted yesterday and it takes at least four days to get there.
Tuesday's meeting was cancelled. I **couldn't have** gone anyway because I was seeing some clients.

THE USE OF CAN'T/COULD/COULDN'T HAVE

Can't have

'Can't have' is used when we think something cannot possibly have happened recently:

The car **can't have** broken down. It was only serviced yesterday.

Could have

'Could have' is used when we describe actions that were possible in the past:

You needn't have got a taxi. I **could have** picked you up in my car. (*But I didn't*).

We **could have** been in serious trouble. (*But we weren't*).

Couldn't have

'Couldn't have' is used when we think something could not possibly have happened in the past:

Steve **couldn't have** authorised that payment. He wasn't working in this department then.

Can't/could/couldn't have followed by the past participle:

CAN'T/COULD/COULDN'T HAVE

It **can't have** **been** Karen that you saw. She's away on holiday.

PAST PARTICIPLE

MODAL VERBS

CAN/COULD

+	I/we/you/they	can	work
	he/she/it	could	

−	I/we/you/they	can't (cannot)	work
	he/she/it	could not (couldn't)	

?	Can	I/we/you/they	work?
	Could	he/she/it	

CAN'T/COULD/COULDN'T HAVE

It	can't have	been	a mistake
	could have		
	couldn't have		

23 May and Might

Possibility

> Interest rates **may** rise in the next few months.

Other examples

We **may** need to increase our prices in the spring.

You **may** be interested in seeing a copy of our new brochure.

Take your winter coat when you go to Russia. It **may** still be very cold in April.

We **might** establish a new plant in Japan in a few years' time, but this is by no means certain.

We don't usually give discounts, but we **might** be able to make an exception in your case for orders of over a thousand dollars.

We **might** be able to help you.

May or might?

'**May**' indicates a stronger possibility than '**might**'.

May	Might
I **may** go to London tomorrow. (It is possible.)	He **might** be here but I haven't seen him yet today. (There is only a slight possibility that he is here.)

Asking for permission (may I/may we...)

"**May** I use your phone, please?"
"Yes, of course you **may**."

Other examples

May I leave early tomorrow, please?
May I interrupt you for a moment?
May I borrow your pen?
May I speak to Susan Jenkins, please?
May we make some suggestions for alterations to your report?
May we point out that we have a special offer on car batteries this month?

(In a letter)
May we draw your attention to paragraph 8 of the enclosed report.

'May' is used in questions with *'I'* and *'we'*.

'Might' is hardly ever used in questions.

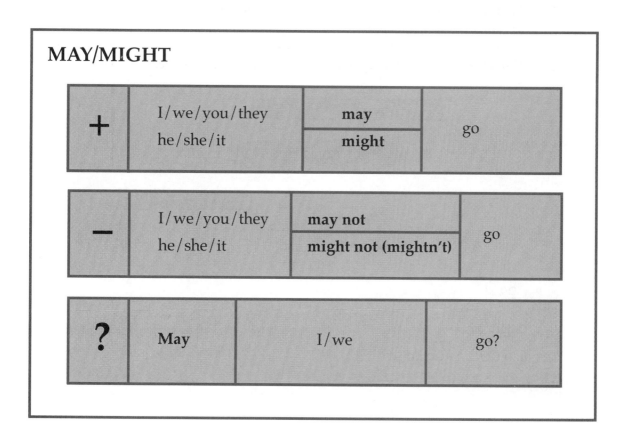

MODAL VERBS

May have and might have

> We were going to start the meeting at nine, but Karl isn't here. He **may not have** received my fax about the change in the time.

Other examples

I can't find my copy of the sales report. I **may have** left it in Tim's office.

I tried to phone my wife, but she isn't there. She **might have** gone shopping.

"Have you received a copy of the auditors' report?"
"I **might have**. There's a pile of things on my desk but I haven't had time to go through them yet."

I expected to hear from Richard today but I haven't. He **may not have** received my message.

Notes

1. *'May have'* and *'might have'* are used to talk about possible happenings in the past. *'May have'* indicates a stronger possibility than *'might have'*:

    He **might have** met their Sales Director, I'm not sure.
    (*There is a slight possibility that he has met him.*)

    He **may have met** their Sales Director before.
    (*There is a reasonable possibility that he has met him before.*)

2. *'May/Might (not) have'* is followed by the past participle:

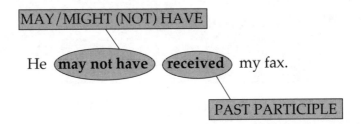

See also *Can and Could* (Unit 22).

24 Must and Have to

Must (obligation)

> If you wish to make a claim on your insurance, you **must** fill in this form as soon as possible.

Other examples

I **must** phone my father. I haven't spoken to him for ages.
Our expenditure was much too high last year. We **must** try to reduce overheads this year.
Requests for a refund **must** be accompanied by a sales receipt.
The new waste disposal measures **must** be ecologically sound.
Payment **must** be received by the end of the month.
Must you leave already? It's still early.

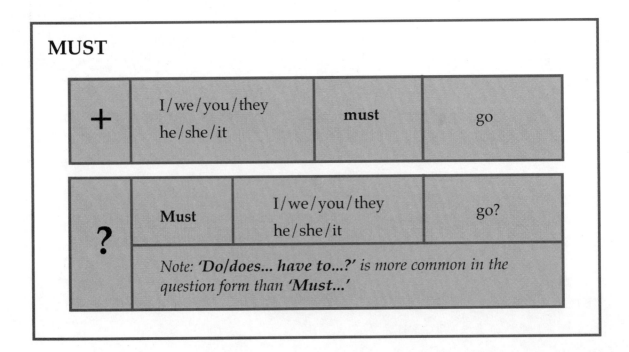

102

GRAMMAR

Have to (obligation)

We have a "flexi-time" system in our company, but all staff **have to** be in the office between the hours of nine-thirty and four-thirty.

Other examples

I'll come out to lunch with you, but I **have to** be back in the office by two o'clock to see the Managing Director.

I'm taking my husband to the doctor's this morning. He **has to** be there early.

We **have to** leave the office by ten o'clock in order to be in time for the meeting at eleven thirty.

The emergency lighting system is faulty. We**'ll have to** get it seen to as soon as we can.

Our car broke down yesterday, so we **had to** take it to the garage.

They **had to** make some minor alterations to the draft advertisement.

Did they **have to** attend the meeting yesterday?

Do you **have to** go to Paris next week?

Must or have to?

1. '**Must**' and '**have to**' are often used in the same way, but there is a slight difference in meaning:

Must	Have to
'**Must**' is often used for **personal obligation**:	'**Have to**' is more **impersonal**:
I **must** hurry. (I think it is necessary to hurry)	I **have to** be at the office at 9 o'clock. (It is a company rule)

2. The past of both '**must**' and '**have to**' is '**had to**':

   I **had to** get up very early yesterday to catch the 6.30 train.

3. '**Must**' and '**have to**' are used both in the present and the future:

   I **must** clean the car tomorrow.
   I **have to** go to a meeting next Friday.

4. '**Will have to**' is also used as the future of both '**must**' and '**have to**':

   I'**ll have to** look at those graphs again before I make my presentation.

MODAL VERBS

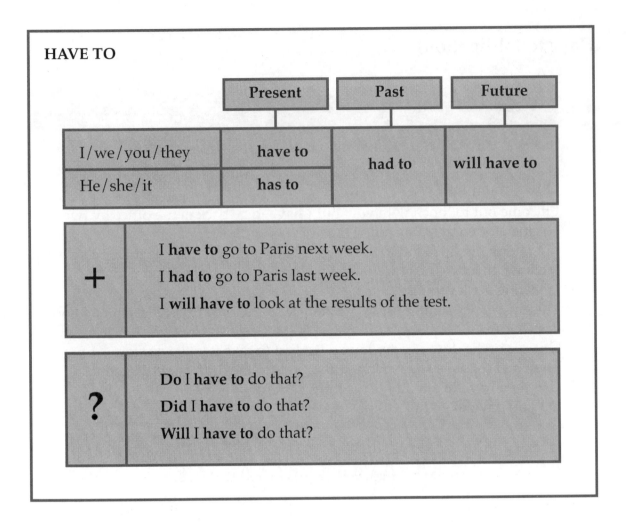

Must be/must have been (deduction)

> "Who's the new person in the Finance Office?"
> "Oh, that **must be** the new accountant. He started today."

Other examples

(Looking at a photograph)
"Who's that standing next to Jim?"
"It **must be** his wife."

"How old is Michael's daughter now?"
"She **must be** about sixteen."

I'm sorry the Sales Director isn't in his office at the moment. He **must be** downstairs in the Accounts Office.

I can't find the file anywhere. My secretary **must have taken** it.
Sally couldn't gain access to the computer system. She **must have forgotten** the password.

Note

'Must be/Must have + past participle' are used when we make a deduction about someone or something:

The letter was posted last week. It **must have arrived** by now.
*(I am not absolutely certain but I **think** it will have arrived).*

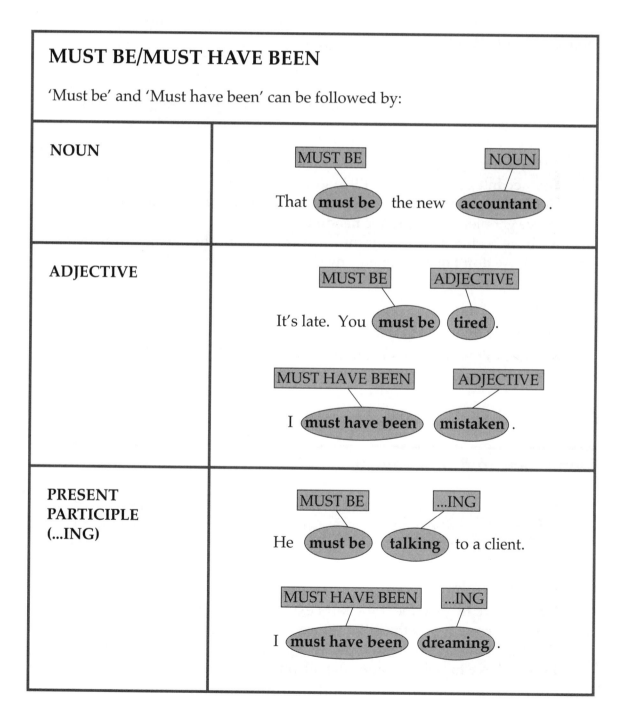

25 Needn't and Mustn't

Needn't/Don't need to

> We **needn't** appoint any new staff to this department until next year.

Other examples
You **needn't** go to the bank. I'll lend you some money.
He **needn't** drive to the party this evening. I'll take him in my car.
We've got plenty of time. We **needn't** hurry.
We have been reviewing our information systems, they are working very well. We **don't need to** make any changes at the moment.

Note
'Needn't'/Don't need to = It is not necessary:
You **needn't** write the report until next week = *It is not necessary to write the report until next week.*

Don't have to/didn't have to

> He lives near the office so he **doesn't have to** take his car to work.

Other examples
I **don't have to** go to the trade fair next week. My colleague is going.
We **don't have to** pay the bill until we have received the full consignment.
Tell Tim he **doesn't have to** type the report. My secretary will do it.
I **didn't have to** write to Jane after all. She phoned me.

Didn't need to

> We **didn't need to** change any of the office equipment last year as it was all fairly new.

Other examples

I **didn't need to** phone James after all because he faxed the information I needed.

You **didn't need to** make any extra copies of the report. I already had enough for distribution.

The company **didn't need to** cut the price as the product was selling well.

Don't/didn't have to/didn't need to

Don't have to

'Don't have to' = don't need to but you can if you wish:

You **don't have to** come early tomorrow.
(But you can come early if you'd like to.)

'Don't have to' and 'needn't' are often used in the same way.
I **don't have to** attend the meeting on Thursday.
I **needn't** attend the meeting on Thursday.

Didn't have to

'Didn't have to' is the **past** form of '**don't have to**'.

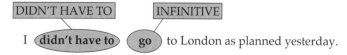

I **didn't have to** **go** to London as planned yesterday.

Didn't need to

'Didn't need to' = the **past** of '**needn't**'.

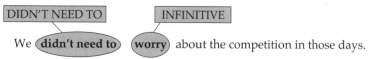

We **didn't need to** **worry** about the competition in those days.

Our products were so much better than those of our competitors.

MODAL VERBS

Needn't have

> "I'm sorry I'm late!"
> "Don't worry. You **needn't have** hurried. We haven't started the meeting yet."

Other examples

I **needn't have** taken my coat. It wasn't cold.

Why did you re-write that proposal? You **needn't have**, the original draft was fine.

I **needn't have** gone to the meeting in London yesterday. My assistant could have dealt with everything for me.

My daughter **needn't have** worried about her examination; she did really well.

I **needn't have** got up so early; the train was late.

Note

'Needn't have' is used if someone did something in the past that was unnecessary:

I needn't have bought so much food. My guests didn't turn up.

(But I had already bought the food as I was expecting the guests to come.)

DIDN'T HAVE TO/DIDN'T NEED TO/NEEDN'T HAVE

Didn't have to/didn't need to

'Didn't have to/didn't need to' are used in the same way:

I **didn't have to** go and see Jill. She came to see me.
I **didn't need to** go and see Jill. She came to see me.

I didn't go

You **didn't have to** type out the whole report again, only the changes.
You **didn't need to** type out the whole report again, only the changes.

But you typed the whole report

didn't have to
or
didn't need to

actions not carried out because it was unnecessary — actions carried out although it was unnecessary

Needn't have

'Needn't have' is only used for actions that have been carried out:

You **needn't have** phoned. I've just sent the information to you by e-mail.

But you did phone

needn't have

actions **carried out** although it was unnecessary

MODAL VERBS

Mustn't (prohibition)

> The report is confidential. You **mustn't** show it to anyone else.

Other examples

We **mustn't** send out the contract until it has been agreed by the legal department.

You **mustn't** smoke in the research laboratory.

He **mustn't** use the car until it has been repaired. It's in a dangerous condition.

Note

'Mustn't' = it is forbidden or it is important not to do something:

In Britain, you **mustn't** park on double yellow lines.
I **mustn't** forget to go to the bank today.

'Mustn't' has no past form. To talk about past prohibition, we use 'was not allowed to' or 'was not permitted to':

I **was not allowed to** smoke when I was a child.

NEEDN'T AND MUSTN'T

PRESENT	PAST
*It is prohibited or it is important **not** to do something*	
mustn't	
It is not necessary	*It was not necessary*
needn't	needn't have
don't need to	didn't need to
don't have to	didn't have to

26 Shall and Should

Suggestions (shall)

> **Shall** we start the meeting by looking back at last year's performance?

Other examples

Shall we begin now?
Shall we go for a drink this evening?
Shall we meet again next Friday?
Shall we go now?

"Are you coming to the shops with me?"
"Yes, **shall** we walk, or take the car?"

Notes

1. *'Shall' is used with 'I' and 'we' to make suggestions:*
   The computer has crashed again. **Shall** I phone for an engineer to come and fix it?

2. *'Shall I' and 'shall we' are followed by the infinitive:*

   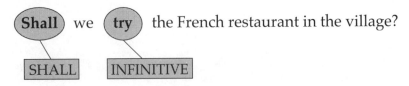

   Shall we try the French restaurant in the village?
   SHALL   INFINITIVE

Offers (shall I?)

> **Shall** I help you to carry those files?

Other examples

Shall I post those letters for you?
Shall I help you with that translation?
It's rather cold in here. **Shall** I shut the window?
Shall I make you a cup of tea?

Advice (should)

> You **should** advertise in the monthly journal; it has a wide readership.

Other examples

You **should** stop smoking, you know. It's bad for your health.
I think you **should** apply for the vacancy in the Marketing Department.
You **should** consider this option very carefully.
You **shouldn't** change the schedule now; everyone's been told about it.
You **should** try going by Underground; it will be much quicker than going by taxi.

See also *Ought to* (Unit 27).

MODAL VERBS

Expectation (should)

The parcel was sent by courier so you **should** receive it tomorrow morning.

Other examples

Bill usually catches the early train so he **should** be here by nine o'clock.
The conference **should** finish by five.
The report **should** be ready by the end of the month.
You **should** receive your goods on Wednesday at the latest.

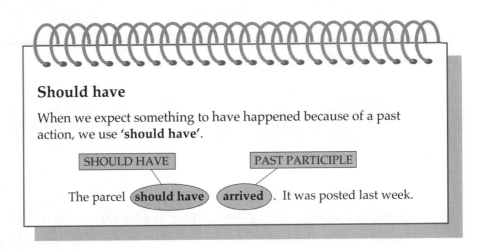

Should have

When we expect something to have happened because of a past action, we use **'should have'**.

SHOULD HAVE   PAST PARTICIPLE

The parcel *should have* *arrived*. It was posted last week.

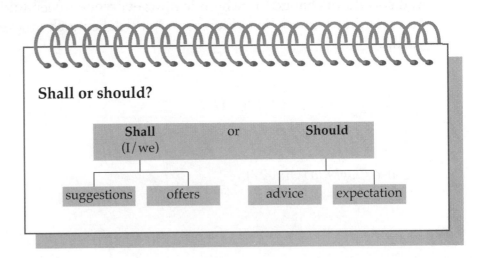

Shall or should?

Shall (I/we) — suggestions, offers
or
Should — advice, expectation

SHALL

+	I/we	**shall ('ll)**	help you
−	I/we	**shall not (shan't)**	help you
?	**Shall**	I/we	help you?

SHOULD

+	I/we/you/they he/she/it	**should**	work
−	I/we/you/they he/she/it	**should not (shouldn't)**	work
?	**Should**	I/we/you/they he/she/it	work?

27 Ought to

Obligation

> Do you think I **ought to** speak to the Purchasing Manager before I order these items?

Other examples
Where's Maurice? He **ought to** be here by now. He's late.
We **ought to** notify the customer that the delivery has been delayed.
Oughtn't you **to** write and thank him for his help?
Ought I **to** show this report to the Managing Director before I send it out?

Note
*To talk about something you should or should not have done **in the past**, use 'ought to have' + past participle:*

I ought to have phoned the suppliers yesterday.

*We can also use **'must'** to express obligation:*
You **must** check those figures very carefully.

'Must' expresses a stronger obligation than 'ought to'.

Advice

> You **oughtn't to** worry so much.

Other examples

We **ought to** speak to David about your car. He's good with engines.
You really **ought to** stay at home at the weekend. You look tired.

Note

'Ought to' is followed by the infinitive:

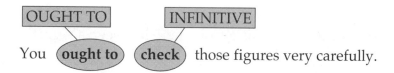

+	I/we/you/they he/she/it	ought to	work
−	I/we/you/they he/she/it	ought not to (oughtn't to)	work
?	Ought	I/we/you/they he/she/it	to work?

See also *Must* (Unit 24) and *Should* (Unit 26)

MODAL VERBS

28 Adjectives and Adverbs

Adjectives

As you can see from this graph, there has been a **significant** increase in productivity over the past few years.

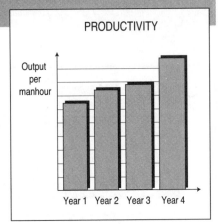

There has been a **significant** increase in productivity

Other examples

James is a **hard** worker.
The new project is very **interesting**.
The delay in production will have a **serious** effect on delivery dates.
There was a **substantial** drop in profits last year.
Did you go to Mr. Svensson's presentation? He's a very **good** speaker.
I didn't go shopping on Saturday because of the **heavy** rain.

Note

*An **adjective** tells us something about a **noun**.*

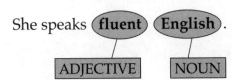

Adjectives ending in ...ed and ...ing: (interested/interesting)

It was an **exciting** football match.
He was very **excited** about the new proposal.

Other examples

The journey was very **tiring**.
He looks very **tired**. He needs a holiday.

Last month's results were quite **surprising**.
Everyone was **surprised** by the results.

...ED AND ...ING

Person A person is (**...ed**)	**Thing** A thing is (**...ing**)
I am **interested** in the project.	The project is **interesting**.
I was **bored** by the film.	The film was **boring**.

!

But we can say:
Linda is an interest**ing** person.
*(The speaker is interest**ed** in Linda.)*

! Typical Error	Correct
~~He was surprising to get the job.~~	He was **surprised** to get the job.

ADJECTIVES AND ADVERBS

Adverbs

> As you can see from the chart, productivity has increased **significantly**.

Other examples
The delay in production will affect our delivery dates **seriously**.
Did you go to Mr. Svensson's presentation? He speaks very **well**.
Profits dropped **substantially** last year.
James works **hard**.
I didn't go shopping on Saturday because it was raining **heavily**.
He spoke so **softly**. I could **hardly** hear him.

Note
*An **adverb** tells us something about a **verb***:

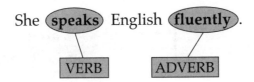

❗ Typical Errors	Correct
~~He drives very good.~~	He drives very **well**.
~~She speaks quiet.~~	She speaks **quietly**.

'Hard' and 'hardly' are different:
He always works **hard** = *He works a lot.*
She has **hardly** any money = *She has almost no money.*

ADJECTIVES AND ADVERBS

Adjectives	Adverbs
bad	badly
careful	carefully
gradual	gradually
significant	significantly
heavy	heavily
easy	easily

Exceptions

good	well
fast	fast

Adverbs modifying adjectives

> We were **bitterly disappointed** not to get the American contract.

Other examples

Jane found the film **really interesting**.
The information they gave us was **slightly misleading**.
The company has had a **very good** start to the year.
The staff canteen provides a **well-balanced** diet.
Our new product is **reasonably priced**.
The service was **barely satisfactory**.

Note

*Some **adverbs** are used to tell us more about an **adjective**:*

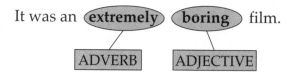

It was an (extremely) (boring) film.
ADVERB   ADJECTIVE

ADJECTIVES AND ADVERBS

⊗ Typical Errors	Correct
~~We need high skilled engineers.~~	We need **highly** skilled engineers.
~~I'm terrible sorry I disturbed you.~~	I'm **terribly** sorry I disturbed you.

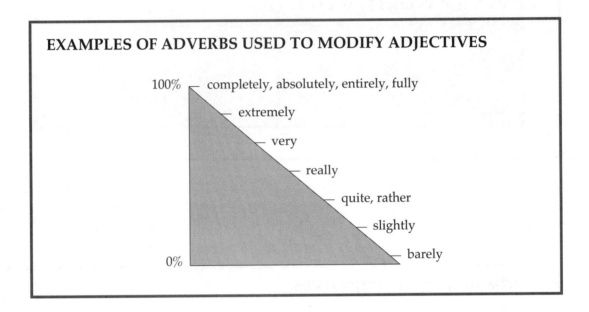

EXAMPLES OF ADVERBS USED TO MODIFY ADJECTIVES

- 100% — completely, absolutely, entirely, fully
- extremely
- very
- really
- quite, rather
- slightly
- 0% — barely

Adverbs modifying adverbs

> The target we set at the beginning of the year was **very easily** achieved.

Other examples

Last week's meeting was arranged **fairly quickly**.
I know the Finance Director of that company **quite well**.
The new machine works **extremely fast**.
Angela drives **very carelessly**.
Although it was a complicated matter, the instructor explained it **quite clearly**.

Note

*Some **adverbs** are used to tell us more about other **adverbs**:*

The sales team performed rather well last month.

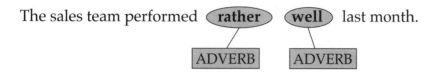

ADVERBS: WORD ORDER

An adverb goes after the verb 'be' but before other verbs:

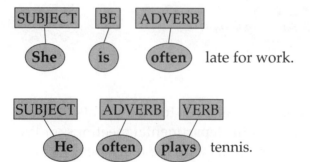

She is often late for work.

He often plays tennis.

An adverb goes between a modal verb and another verb:

It will probably rain tomorrow.

An adverb can go before another adverb:

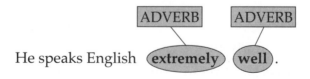

He speaks English extremely well.

An adverb can go before an adjective:

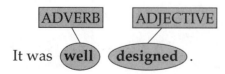

It was well designed.

ADJECTIVES AND ADVERBS

29 Frequency Adverbs

How often?

> He **usually** goes to work by car.

Other examples

They **always** send Christmas cards to their clients.
We **nearly always** hold our departmental meetings on Tuesdays.
We **sometimes** have problems with the machines.
Tom **occasionally** has to work at weekends.
He **rarely** travels abroad.
We used to be great friends but we **hardly ever** meet now as we live so far apart.
I **never** drink coffee in the evening as it keeps me awake.
How often do you go skiing?

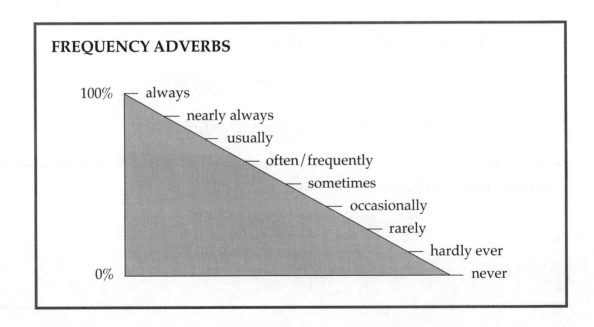

FREQUENCY ADVERBS

- 100% — always
- nearly always
- usually
- often / frequently
- sometimes
- occasionally
- rarely
- hardly ever
- 0% — never

Frequency adverbs: word order

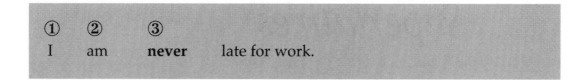

①	②	③	
I	am	**never**	late for work.

Other examples

①	②	③	
He	is	**often**	in France.
Jane	**always**	plays	tennis at the weekend.
We	**usually**	go	shopping on Saturdays.

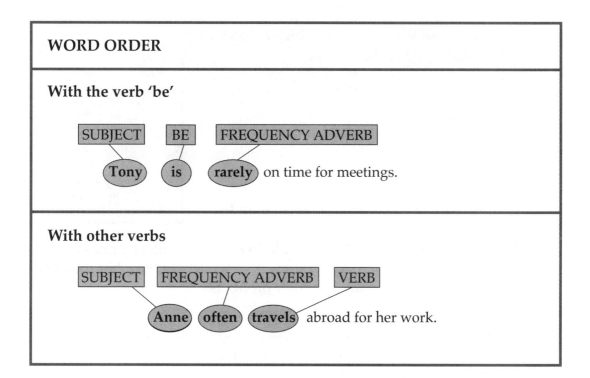

WORD ORDER

With the verb 'be'

SUBJECT — BE — FREQUENCY ADVERB

Tony is **rarely** on time for meetings.

With other verbs

SUBJECT — FREQUENCY ADVERB — VERB

Anne **often** travels abroad for her work.

See also *Present Simple* (Unit 1), and *Adjectives and Adverbs* (Unit 28).

30 Comparatives and Superlatives

Comparison of adjectives

> Interest rates are two per cent **higher** than they were at this time last year.

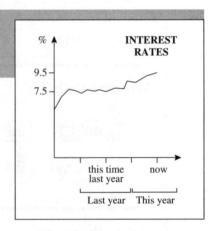

Interest rates are two per cent **higher** than last year.

Other examples

She finds it **easier** to write in English than to speak it.
He's got a bad cold but he's getting **better**.
Profits were **higher** than expected.
They are a **larger** company and their products are **more expensive** than ours.

This photocopier is **more reliable** than the one in my office.
My new car has a **more powerful** engine than the old one.
This project is getting **more and more interesting.**

He makes **less** money than he used to.
This project is **less interesting** than the previous one.

Notes

1. *We normally use 'than' after comparatives:*
   He's worked for the company for **longer than** anyone else.

2. *'As...as' is sometimes used when making a comparison:*
   This machine is twice **as** expensive **as** the one we looked at yesterday.
   The instructions in the manual are not **as** clear **as** they could be.

126 GRAMMAR

3. *Comparing ages*: the comparative of *'old'* is *'older'* which can be used for people and things. *'Elder'* is used only for people: "Mark is Catherine's **elder** brother" but we cannot say *'elder than'*.

> **The + comparative + the + comparative**
>
> We use **'the + comparative + the + comparative'** when one comparative is the result of another:
>
> **The cheaper** the production costs, **the more** profit we will make.
> **The earlier** we leave, **the sooner** we'll arrive.

Degrees of comparison

Our profits last year were **considerably lower** than the year before.

Other examples

Costs will be **substantially higher** next year.
His workload is **much heavier** than mine.
Demand for this product is **significantly greater** than it was last year.
The economic situation is **moderately better** now.

Note

Adverbs are used before comparative adjectives to show degrees of comparison:

The weather is *slightly better* today. It's not quite so windy.

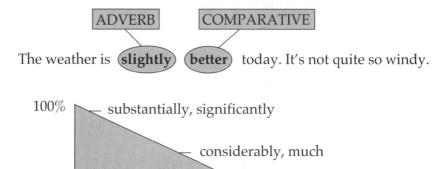

ADJECTIVES AND ADVERBS

Superlatives (adjectives)

What is **the most interesting** job you have ever had?

Other examples

This is **the cheapest** product of its kind on the market.
This is **the best** and **most efficient** printer we have ever had.
I'm sorry, Tuesday is **the worst** possible day for me. Can we meet on Wednesday instead?
It was **the most interesting** presentation I have heard on that subject.
It was **the least enjoyable** party I have ever been to.
Coca Cola is **the most successful** soft drinks manufacturer, and they have **the biggest share** of the market.

Notes

1. *'The' is normally used before a superlative:*

   Everest is **the highest** mountain in the world.

2. *We often use the Present Perfect and Past Perfect after a superlative:*

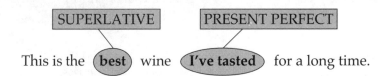

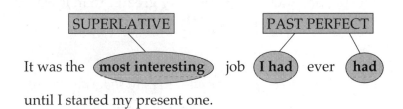

until I started my present one.

See also *Present Perfect* (Unit 6) and *Past Perfect* (Unit 8).

3. ***Comparing ages***: *the superlative of 'old' is 'oldest' which can be used for both people and things. 'Eldest' is used only for people.*

   Henry has three sons. The **eldest** is a doctor.

COMPARATIVES AND SUPERLATIVES: ADJECTIVES

One-syllable adjectives

cheap	cheaper	cheapest
high	higher	highest
near	nearer	nearest
few	fewer	fewest

Some two-syllable adjectives take '-er' and '-est'

clever	cleverer	cleverest
quiet	quieter	quietest

Two-syllable adjectives that end in '-y' take '-ier' and '-iest'

early	earlier	earliest
easy	easier	easiest

Many two-syllable adjectives take 'more' and 'most'

careful	more careful	most careful
modern	more modern	most modern

Three- and four-syllable adjectives

expensive	more expensive	most expensive
interesting	more interesting	most interesting
profitable	more profitable	most profitable

Exceptions

good	better	best
bad	worse	worst
much/many	more	most
little	less	least

ADJECTIVES AND ADVERBS

Comparison of adverbs

> You didn't understand what he was trying to tell you. You should listen **more carefully** to what he has to say.

Other examples

Can you explain again, a little **more slowly**, please?
You'll learn how to use the new computer program **more easily** if you read the instruction manual.
I think we are disturbing the people in the next room. Perhaps we should speak **more quietly**.
He works **harder** than his brother does.
The product performed much **worse** than expected.

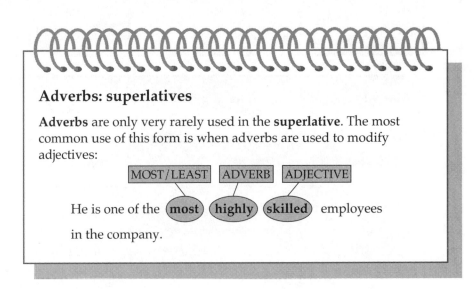

See also *Comparing and Contrasting* (Unit 58).

COMPARATIVES AND SUPERLATIVES: ADVERBS

Adverbs

quickly	more quickly	most quickly
efficiently	more efficiently	most efficiently

Exceptions

hard	harder	hardest
fast	faster	fastest
well	better	best
badly	worse	worst

31 Reported Speech

Useful reporting verbs

> The Chairman **stated** that the company had returned to profitability.

Other examples

James **informed** me (that) he wouldn't be able to attend the meeting on Monday.
He **asked** me whether I would like to have dinner with him.
They **agreed** to give us a ten per cent discount on all our orders.
I **explained** to the customer that we wouldn't be able to despatch his order for another two weeks.
Janet **said** she had been to Greece for her holidays.
He **told** me that he worked for Siemens.
He **complained** that the contractors had not followed safety procedures.

Note

In some sentences, 'that' can be omitted:

The Accounts Supervisor **suggested** (that) we should buy two more laser printers for the office.

Useful reporting verbs:

ask	agree	announce	complain	declare
explain	inform	notify	reply	report
say	state	suggest	tell	

Changing from direct to indirect (reported) speech

Direct speech	Indirect (reported) speech
"I worked for a company in Pamplona for two years."	She **said** (that) she **had worked** for a company in Pamplona for two years.

Other examples

Direct speech	Indirect (reported) speech
"Have you ever been to Poland?"	He **asked** me if I **had** ever **been** to Poland. *or* He **wanted to know** if I **had** ever **been** to Poland.
"I can't come to the conference. I'm very busy."	She **told** me she **couldn't** come to the conference as she **was** very busy.

Tense changes

Usually, **present** tenses change to **past** tenses in reported speech, for example:

is	was
have	had
can	could
will	would, etc.

The tense does **not** change when the words spoken are still true, and we sometimes also use the present tense for the reporting verbs.

| "We'll hold the meeting next week." | He said (or says) they**'ll** hold the meeting next week. |
| "Profits are much higher this year." | She said (or says) that profits **are** much higher this year. |

CLAUSES

DIRECT SPEECH		INDIRECT SPEECH
Present Simple "I **work** in London." "What time **does** the meeting **begin**?"		*Past Simple* He said (that) he **worked** in London. She wanted to know what time the meeting **began**.
Present Continuous "I**'m staying** at the Grand Hotel."		*Past Continuous* She told me (that) she **was staying** at the Grand Hotel.
Present Perfect "I**'ve worked** here for ten years."		*Past Perfect* He told me (that) he **had worked** there for ten years.
Will "I**'ll** see you tomorrow."		*Would* He said he **would** see me the following day.
Can "**Can** you write to the contractors?"		*Could* He asked if I **could** write to the contractors.
Past Simple "I **worked** in London twenty years ago."		*Past Simple or Past Perfect* She told me she **worked** in London twenty years previously/ago. *or* She told me she **had worked**...

Reported speech and time phrases

Direct speech	Indirect (reported) speech
"We signed the contract last week."	She told me they had signed the contract **the previous week.**

Other examples

Direct speech	Indirect (reported) speech
"Negotiations between the two countries took place last month."	The minister reported that negotiations between the two countries had taken place **the previous month.**

*In reported speech, time phrases sometimes remain the same as they are in direct speech. For example if someone tells me something this week and I tell someone else during the same week, the time phrase **does not** change.*

"I'll phone you **next week**." He says he'll phone me **next week**.

If next week is no longer an appropriate phrase, and we are reporting this at a much later date, we change it like this:

He said he would phone me **the following week**.

CHANGES TO TIME PHRASES

When reporting something at a later date, we change the time phrases.

Direct speech	Indirect (reported) speech
today	that day
tomorrow	the following day / the day after
yesterday	the previous day / the day before
this (Saturday)	that (Saturday)
next (Saturday)	the following (Saturday)
last (Saturday)	the previous (Saturday)

CLAUSES

Reported questions

Direct speech	Indirect (reported) speech
"When will you send me the results?"	He **asked** me when I **would** send him the results.

Other examples

Direct speech	Indirect (reported) speech
"Will you be able to attend the meeting next week?"	She **asked** me **whether** I **would** be able to attend the meeting the following week.
"Have you checked the draft contract?"	Sheila **wanted to know if** I **had checked** the draft contract.
"Where do you buy your raw materials?"	He **wanted to know where** we **bought** our raw materials.

Note

1. *Open questions (what, when, where, who, whose, which, how):*

    "(**How**) are you getting to France?"

    He asked me (**how**) I was getting to France.

2. *Closed questions (questions requiring "Yes/No" answers):*

    "(**Does**) your department deal with invoices?"

    He asked me (**if/whether**) my department deals/dealt with invoices.

3. *Requests:*

    "Can you (**give**) this to the manager, please?"

    She asked me (**to give**) it to the manager.

Commands and warnings

Direct speech	Indirect (reported) speech
"Check all the stock very carefully and count the number of damaged items."	His boss **told him to check** all the stock very carefully and **to count** the number of damaged items.

Other examples

Direct speech	Indirect (reported) speech
"You mustn't park there. That space is reserved for the Chief Executive."	**He told** me **not to park** in the Chief Executive's space.
"Don't lean on the balcony. It's not safe!"	**She warned** me **not to lean** on the balcony.

Note

1. We *'tell'* or *'ask'* somebody *'to do'* something, or *'not to do'* something:

2. We *'warn'* somebody *'not to do'* something:

    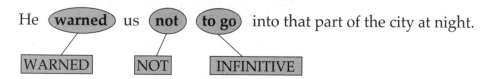

In English, a command is sometimes given in the form of a question:
"Would/will you give this to Mr. Simpson?" *said by a boss to an employee is really a command!*

32 Time Clauses

What are time clauses?

> **As soon as I get any news from our solicitors**, I'll phone you.

Other examples
Having finished the meeting, they went home.
After doing the shopping, we went for a coffee.
Whenever taxes are increased, consumer spending falls.
While I'm in Washington, I hope to meet the Ambassador.

Notes

1. A *clause* is a group of words (with a subject and a verb) which forms a sentence or part of a sentence. A *clause* often also has an object:

2. A *time clause* is added to other parts of a sentence to tell us when something happens or happened.

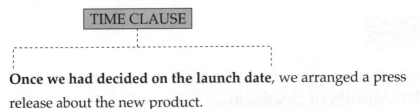

Once we had decided on the launch date, we arranged a press release about the new product.

138 GRAMMAR

3. The **time clause** can also be the second clause in the sentence:

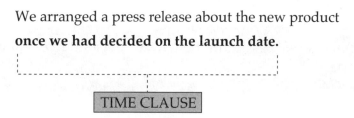

Whenever, while, as

> **While** you were in the meeting, the Managing Director came looking for you.

Other examples
Whenever we have a meeting, George arrives late.
It rains **whenever** I go to Scotland.
I arrived at the station just **as** the train was leaving.

Note
'While' and *'as'* are used to talk about two events that happen **at the same time**.
While I was trying to phone you, your fax arrived on my desk.

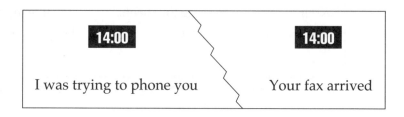

'Whenever' = *every time.*

CLAUSES

After, before, as soon as, since

After being so successful in the UK, we decided to expand into the rest of Europe.

Other examples

Before agreeing to your suggestions, we should like to clarify a few points.
As soon as the meeting had finished, he left for the airport.
Many changes have been made **since** he became Finance Director.
There are one or two details we'd like to discuss **before** finalising our agreement.

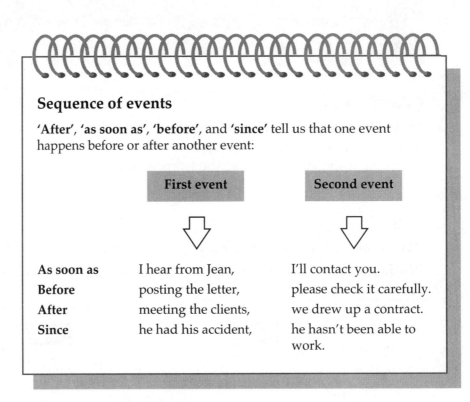

Sequence of events

'After', 'as soon as', 'before', and 'since' tell us that one event happens before or after another event:

	First event	Second event
As soon as	I hear from Jean,	I'll contact you.
Before	posting the letter,	please check it carefully.
After	meeting the clients,	we drew up a contract.
Since	he had his accident,	he hasn't been able to work.

Having + past participle

We can also use **'having'** and the **'past participle'** in a **'time clause'** to show that one event happens before another one:

Having considered all the bids, we decided to use the Scottish company as our main contractor.

!

This is more common in written than in spoken English.

See also *Past Continuous* (Unit 4), *Present Perfect* (Unit 6) and *Past Perfect* (Unit 8).

33 Relative Clauses

What are relative clauses?

> Hans Groot, **who is the Accounts Manager**, is now based at the Rotterdam office.

Other examples

The message **that you sent to Mr. Wilson** didn't reach him until late in the afternoon.

Nils Jacobsen, **who used to be in charge of sales**, has been replaced by Pekka Fridén.

The ideas **that he discussed in his presentation** have given us a lot to think about.

The report **that you wrote** was very interesting.

Note

A clause is a group of words which form part of a sentence.

A relative clause is joined to the rest of the sentence with 'who', 'which', 'where', 'that', 'when' and 'whose'. It tells us which person or object is being referred to:

My brother works for a company **which designs software.** [RELATIVE CLAUSE]

The book **that you gave me for my birthday** is very interesting. [RELATIVE CLAUSE]

Defining and non-defining relative clauses

Defining relative clauses

> The customer **who complained about the delay** is demanding a refund.

I don't want to reveal the identity of the person **who gave me the information**.
We cannot give discounts on orders **which need to be despatched at short notice**.
I have seen the film **that you recommended to us**. It is very good.

Non-defining relative clauses

> The conference hotel, **which is very modern**, is in the centre of the city.

James Merriott, **who lives next door**, works in publishing.
My brother, **who lives in Hamburg**, is an accountant.

DEFINING RELATIVE CLAUSES	NON-DEFINING RELATIVE CLAUSES
These give us essential information to identify the person or thing that is being spoken about	*These give us non-essential information (If it were omitted, the main message of the sentence would remain clear)*
The person **who deals with credit control** is not in the office at the moment.	Sylvia Burton, **with whom I discussed the project**, likes the idea.
(There are no commas with these clauses)	*(Notice the commas around this type of clause)*

CLAUSES

People: who, whom, whose

> (On the telephone)
> I'd like to speak to the person **(who is*) responsible for sending out invoices.**

Other examples

The person **who can help you with your query** is Jane Smith in the Customer Services Department.

The other two people **with whom I worked on that project** have now left the company.

The woman **I was speaking to just now** is the Sales Director.

I should like to introduce you to Mr. Bryant, **who is an expert in chemical engineering.**

Maria Hernandez, **(who is*) my secretary**, will meet you at the airport.

* *In this type of sentence 'who is' can be left out.*

Using 'whom' and 'whose'

1. **'Whom'** is normally only used in a **very formal** context.
   George Appleby is the person to **whom** the letter should be sent.

   It is more common in spoken English to say:
   George Appleby is the person you should send the letter to.

2. **'Whose'** is used for possessives:
   The Marketing Manager, **whose** car had broken down, was late for the meeting.

Objects: which, that

> The new offices, **which will accommodate about fifty people**, are being decorated at the moment.

Other examples

The information **(that) we get from Head Office** is often too late to be of much use to us.

We have run out of stock and have ordered five thousand more units, **which will be delivered on Friday**.

Using 'which' and 'that'

'Which' or 'that' are used in relative clauses about things.

The restaurant **which/that** we normally go to is the Italian one on the corner of Madison Street.

In this type of sentence, it is also possible to leave out **'which'** or **'that'**:

The restaurant we normally go to is the Italian one on the corner of Madison Street.

34 Prepositions: Introduction

There are three units on prepositions. They are:

Verbs and Prepositions   Unit 35
Nouns and Prepositions   Unit 36
Prepositions and Nouns   Unit 37

The prepositions in these units are listed below:

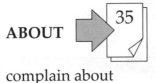

ABOUT

complain about
hear about
think about

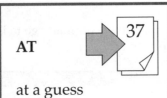

AT

at a guess
at all costs
at first glance
at last
at once
at the latest

BY

by chance, accident
by cheque
by credit card
by mistake

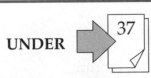

UNDER

under control
under discussion
under review
under way

146   GRAMMAR

FOR

apologise for
apply for
pay for
prepare for
wait for

demand for
need for
reason for
respect for

for a change
for a drink, a meal
for example
for a meeting
for a swim, a walk

IN

delay in
decrease/fall in
difficulty in
increase/rise in

in advance
in agreement
in cash
in charge
in confidence
in... opinion
in practice
in principle
in the end
in theory
in time
in writing

OF

approve of
consist of
think of

account of
advantage of
cause of
cost of
depth of
disadvantage of
height of
length of
opinion of
rate of
result of
speed of
way of
weight of

ON

agree on
concentrate on
depend on
insist on
rely on

on business
on holiday
on the agenda
on the telephone
on time

TO

belong to
complain to
object to
respond/reply to

answer/reply to
attitude to
demand to
invitation to
reaction to
solution to

WITH

agree with
supply with

connection with
contact with
difficulty with
relationship with

35 Verbs + Prepositions

About

> Have you **heard** the news **about** Robin? He's been promoted.

Other examples

"Did you have a good trip to Paris?"
"Yes. The meeting went well but the hotel was terrible. I had to **complain about** the room."

What does Peter **think about** our chances of doing more business in Italy?

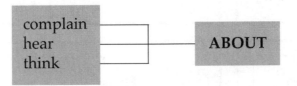

Hear about/hear from

We **'hear about'** something or someone, but if we receive a letter or a phone call, we **'hear from'** someone:

We look forward to **hearing from** you soon.

For

> Our suppliers have **apologised for** their mistake and they have promised to give us a credit note.

Other examples

Over fifty people **applied for** the vacant post in the production department.
How much did you have to **pay for** the compact disks?
I don't want to be disturbed this afternoon; I've got to **prepare for** the board meeting next week.
I have asked the bank for a new cheque book, but we are still **waiting for** them to send it to us.

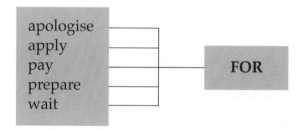

Pay

We pay someone **'for'** something but we **pay a bill, pay taxes**, etc.:
I've checked out and **paid the bill**.

Apply to/for

We apply to someone or to a company **'for'** a job:
He applied to Browns **for** the job in Sales.

PREPOSITIONS

Of

> We don't **approve of** what the Government is doing to the health service.

Other examples

The training course will **consist of** lectures, group work and individual projects.

This is your first visit to Amsterdam, isn't it? What do you **think of** it?

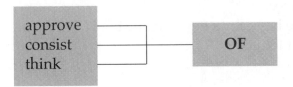

Think of/think about

1. 'Think of' something = to have an idea:
   I wish I'd **thought of** that!

2. 'Think of' or 'think about' = to have an opinion or to consider:

   To have an opinion:
   What did you **think of** Philip's idea?
   What did you **think about** Philip's idea?

   To consider:
   I'm **thinking of** changing my car soon.
   I'm **thinking about** changing my car soon.

On

> We have **agreed on** a course of action that should help the company to recover its leading position on the market.

Other examples

I'm finding it very difficult to **concentrate on** my work with all that building work going on outside!

Whether we develop that particular product line or not **depends on** the results of the market research survey.

I must **insist on** absolute secrecy about this new project. Our competitors must not get to hear about it.

Why don't you ask Janet to do that job for you? You can **rely on** her.

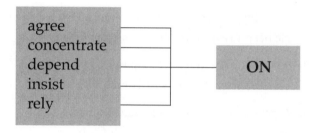

To

> I have **complained to** their Customer Service Manager about the late delivery of the goods I ordered from them.

Other examples

Who does this briefcase **belong to**? It seems to have been left behind by someone.

He hasn't **replied to** my letter yet.

"How did the negotiations go?"
"Well, they didn't **object to** our suggestions and we managed to reach a satisfactory agreement."

PREPOSITIONS

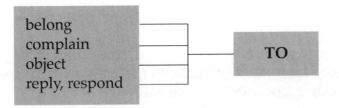

To

1. We complain **'to'** someone **about** something:
   I complained **to** the hotel manager **about** the poor central heating.

2. We reply or **'respond to'** **a person, a letter,** or **a suggestion**:
   He hasn't **responded to** my suggestion yet.

3. Something **'belongs to'** **someone**:
   That briefcase **belongs to** Tom Smith.

4. A person **'belongs to'** an **organisation**:
   Ian **belongs to** Kingsdown Golf Club.
   I **belong to** the Institute of Chartered Surveyors.

5. We **'object to'** something:
   I **objected to** his rude behavior.

With

That's an excellent idea. I **agree with** you completely.

Other examples

"How many boxes would you like?"
"Well. Can you **supply** us **with** about fifty?"

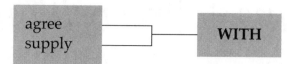

*We **supply** someone **'with'** something, but we **supply** something **'to'** someone:*
The company **supplies** schools **with** educational books.
The company **supplies** educational books **to** schools.

Agree on/agree to/agree with

We **'agree with'** someone, but we **'agree to do'** something, and we **'agree on'** an idea.

I said that we should spend more on computer hardware. He **agreed with** me.

I **agreed to** go with my Sales Director to Brussels to meet our new customer.

We discussed how we should try to improve the morale of our staff and **agreed on** a plan of action.

36 Nouns + Prepositions

For

> Market research shows that there is a great **demand for** this kind of product.

Other examples
There is a **need for** young, highly qualified engineers.
Let me explain the **reasons for** the proposed staffing changes.
I have great **respect for** David Lloyd's opinions. He's always very sensible.

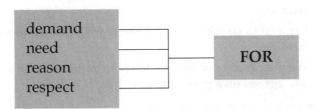

In

> There has been a significant **increase in** bank lending since last year.

Other examples
We must apologise for the **delay in** contacting you.
We have experienced great **difficulty in** finding a suitable person to fill the vacant post in the production department.

The **fall in** demand was largely due to the recession.

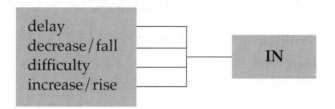

Of

During my presentation, I'll give a brief **account of** the department's activities over the last year.

Other examples

One **advantage of** having a branch in Vienna is the proximity of some other countries we are interested in, such as Hungary and the Czech Republic.

This machine broke down yesterday, but the technician managed to find the **cause of** the problem and he mended it.

The **cost of** the new building could run into millions of dollars.

What's your **opinion of** the architect's plans for the new extension?

Our share of the market has increased steadily at a **rate of** about two per cent each year.

What was the **result of** your meeting yesterday, Martin?

I was driving at a **speed of** about forty kilometres per hour when the accident happened.

Let's try a different **way of** dealing with this problem.

The **weight of** the package is five kilos.

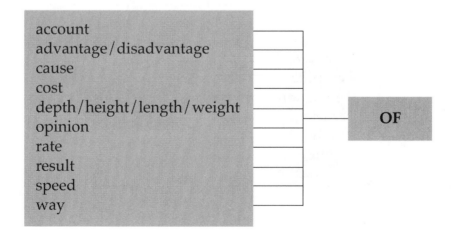

PREPOSITIONS

Advantage of/advantage in

We say: "An advantage **of** being based in the south of England is that we are able to get to London easily."

but

we say: "There is an advantage **in** doing something."

There are two main advantages **in** opening a new factory in Mexico; one is the low cost of labour, the other is proximity to the North American Market.

To

Their initial **reaction to** the rise in interest rates was one of concern about its effect on the exchange rate.

Other examples

Could you let us have an **answer to** these questions by Friday?

I am very impressed with Andrew. He seems to have a very positive **attitude to** the job.

The **invitations to** the reception were sent out yesterday.

I haven't received a **reply to** the letter I sent to Harrisons.

Do you think we can find a **solution to** the technical problems by the end of this month?

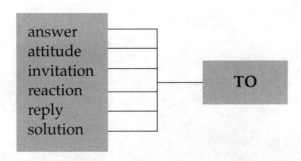

With

> I am phoning in **connection with** your recent enquiry regarding our products.

Other examples

Have you had much **contact with** the advertising agency since the advertising campaign ended?

Can you help me with this translation, please? I'm having some **difficulty with** it.

We have a good **relationship with** our main customers. Our sales representatives visit them regularly.

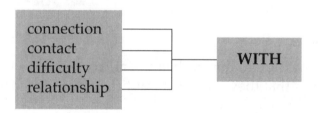

With or between? With or in?

1. **Contact/relationship between**
   'Contact' and 'relationship' are also used with 'between':
   There has been no **contact between** us for over a year.
   There is a good **relationship between** the manager and his staff.

2. **Difficulty with/difficulty in**
   We say '**difficulty with something**' but '**difficulty in doing something**':
   We had some **difficulty in finding** all the information we needed.

37 Prepositions + Nouns

At

> I should be grateful if you would reply by the end of December **at the latest**.

Other examples

We must find a solution to this problem **at all costs**.
At a guess, I'd say that they'll need about fifty copies of the report but I'll check the number tomorrow.
At first glance, the results look disappointing, but if you compare them with last year's results, they are not so bad.
We've received payment from the customer **at last**!
We must start work on this report **at once**.

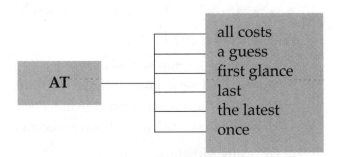

AT — all costs / a guess / first glance / last / the latest / once

By

> (In a shop/restaurant)
> "How would you like to pay, Madam?"
> "**By credit card**, please."

Other examples

I saw Roger Davis yesterday. I bumped into him **by chance** in the street.
I think this is your pen. I picked it up **by mistake** yesterday.

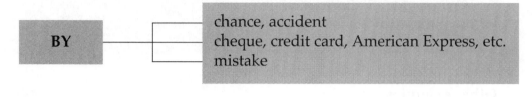

We pay 'in' cash.

For

They have decided to hold this year's management conference in the UK **for a change**. They usually hold it in Germany.

Other examples

Would you like to come round **for a drink** this evening?
Geoff's going to London **for a meeting** tomorrow.
Jim likes to go **for a swim** every morning before breakfast.
There are a lot of beautiful cities in central Europe, Prague, **for example**.

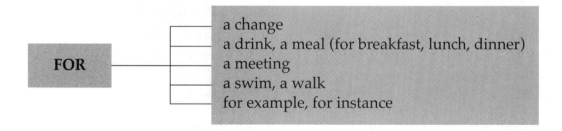

In

> (In a shop or restaurant)
> "How would you like to pay, sir?"
> "**In cash**, please."

Other examples

You'll have to pay for the goods **in advance**.
Well, I think we're all **in agreement**, so perhaps we can go on to the next point.
George's deputy is **in charge** of the department while he's away.
I'm telling you this **in confidence**. Please don't tell anyone else at the moment.
I agree with the proposal **in principle**, but I disagree with some of the details.
In my opinion, we should freeze salaries for the next year as a cost-cutting measure.

"How did the negotiations go yesterday?"
"Well, the discussions went on for a long time, but we reached agreement **in the end**."

"You left rather late yesterday. Were you **in time** for the meeting?"
"Yes, I was. I got there about half an hour early!"

It's a good idea **in theory**, but I don't think it'll work **in practice**.
He agreed to give us a fifteen per cent discount when I spoke to him yesterday, but we must make sure that he puts his offer **in writing**.

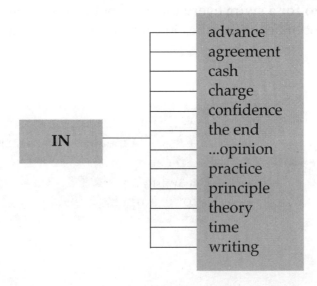

Notes

1. We say *'in'* cash' but *'by'* cheque, credit card, American Express, etc.
2. *'In the end'* = finally, after waiting a long time,
   but we say *'at the end of'* a conversation, a meeting, a report, book, etc.

On

"Hello, Mr Parsons. I haven't seen you lately."
"No. I've just come back from Paris."
"Oh. Were you there **on holiday** or **on business**?"
"**On business**."

Other examples

"Is Jane in the office today?"
"Yes, but she's **on the telephone** at the moment."

We must start the meeting exactly **on time** tomorrow. There are a lot of items **on the agenda**.

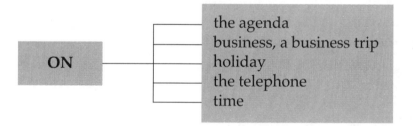

On time/in time

'**On time**' = punctual, exactly at the right time.

'**In time**' = early, before the start of something for example, "**in time** for the meeting."

On holiday/for a holiday

We say that someone is **'on'** holiday but we can also say that someone goes somewhere **'for'** a holiday:

He is **on holiday** in Venice.
Keith's gone to Spain **for his holiday**.

PREPOSITIONS

Under

> There has been a riot by demonstrators in the street today, but the police have the situation **under control**.

Other examples

We haven't made a decision yet about our capital expenditure programme. The matter is **under discussion**.

Our current production systems are **under review**. We might decide to introduce some changes.

The market research study is now **under way**, and should be completed by the end of the month.

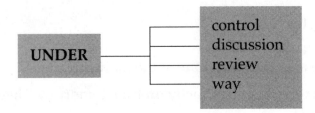

Note

Under way = going on

PREPOSITIONS

38 Countable and Uncountable Nouns

Countable Nouns

> We're installing **a** new **machine** in the factory next month.

Singular

Would you like **a cup** of tea?
A scanner is a useful item of equipment.
That's **a** beautiful **piece** of music.
Could you buy **a loaf** of bread for me, please?
Have you got **a car**?

Plural

They are going to buy **some** new **computers** for the accounts department.
He gave me **two copies** of the report.
She has **three brothers**.
There are **some letters** for you on the desk.
I'm meeting **some friends** on Saturday.
Have you read **any** good **books** recently?

Countable Nouns are used in the singular and the plural and can be counted with numbers.

Singular	Plural
a book, one book	two books, three books
a man, one man	two men, three men
a child, one child	two children, three children
a company, one company	two companies, a group of companies

We can use 'a' or 'an' before singular countable nouns:

a job
an orange

Countable nouns with 'some' and 'any'

1. We use **'some'** with countable nouns in the **'plural'**:
   I must buy **some** new **shoes**.

2. **'Any'** is often used in questions and negatives with countable nouns in the **'plural'**:
   Have you got **any cigarettes**?
   There aren't **any letters** for you today.

See also *Some and Any* (Unit 40) and *Quantity* (Unit 41).

Uncountable Nouns

We're installing **some** new **machinery** in the factory next month.

Other examples

Would you like **some tea**?
There's a lot of expensive computer **equipment** in the office.
I love listening to classical **music**.
Could you buy **some bread** for me, please?
Could you give me **some information** about your prices, please?
Have you got **any time** tomorrow to discuss my ideas for the Paris meeting?

Uncountable nouns:
1. *have only one form (examples: information, music, work, happiness)*
2. *cannot be counted with numbers*
3. *take a singular verb*

Advertising **is** an expensive way for us to market our goods.
(UNCOUNTABLE NOUN / SINGULAR VERB)

Uncountable nouns with 'some' and 'any'

1. **Uncountable nouns** are never used with **'a'** or **'an'**. They are often used with **'some'**:

   He gave me **some** advice.

   In sentences like this, **'some'** is not used:

   Do you like **wine**?

2. **'Any'** is often used in questions and negatives with uncountable nouns:

   Is there **any money** in the petty cash float?
   There isn't **any coffee** left.

! Typical Error	Correct
~~Could you give me some informations, please?~~	Could you give me some **information**, please?

COUNTABLE AND UNCOUNTABLE NOUNS

COUNTABLE NOUNS	UNCOUNTABLE NOUNS
can be counted	**cannot** be counted
Singular	**Singular**
a/an **one (1)** — company, machine, man	machinery, information, money, advice, advertising
Plural	
some **2, 3, 4, 5** — companies, machines, men	! Uncountable nouns take a **singular** verb: TV advertising **is** expensive.

See also *Some and Any* (Unit 40) and *Quantity* (Unit 41).

NOUNS

167

39 Articles (a/an/the)

A/an (indefinite article)

> A company is a subsidiary if it is owned by another company.

Other examples
They live in a small house in the centre of the city.
Do you think the Hilton Hotel would be a suitable venue for the conference?
They made a loss of one million pounds last year.
We received an estimate for the building work this morning.
I read an article about the Bundesbank in the Financial Times yesterday.

Note
The indefinite article 'a'/'an' is used with countable nouns in the singular:

INDEFINITE ARTICLE — COUNTABLE NOUN IN SINGULAR

I watched (a) (programme) on TV about terrorism in Europe.

The (definite article)

> Industry is gradually recovering from **the** economic recession.

Other examples

Logica designs computer software. **The** company is based in London.
Marks and Spencer is one of **the** most successful British retailing companies.
I found **the** recommendations in your report very interesting.
There isn't a bank in my village. **The** nearest bank is about ten miles away.
We will need to put a proposal to **the** board of directors.
Austria joined **the** European Union in 1995.

When do we use 'the'?

The definite article **'the'** is used:

1. when we speak about something we have already mentioned:

    I paid a cheque into the bank today. **The** cheque was from the insurance company.

2. when we expect the listener to understand what we are referring to:

    The meeting has been postponed until next week.
    (The listener knows which meeting is being referred to.)

3. when we talk about something specific:

    The water in many Scandinavian rivers is polluted by acid rain.
    (The water is **specific**.)

    You will find **the information on page twelve** very helpful.
    (The information is **specific**.)

4. when there is only **'one'** particular thing:

    Helsinki is **the** capital of Finland.
    (There is only **one** capital in Finland.)

    We flew across **the** Atlantic Ocean.
    (There is only **one** Atlantic Ocean.)

DETERMINERS

No article (the zero article)

Cars parked without permission will be clamped.

Other examples

Information on all our products can be found in the enclosed brochure.
Petrol is getting more and more expensive.
Do you have **cable television** at home?

When is there no article?

No article (the zero article) is used with:

1. Countable nouns in the plural (when they are not specific)

   COUNTABLE NOUN IN PLURAL

   Club members receive discounts on flights within Europe.

2. Uncountable nouns (when they are not specific)

   UNCOUNTABLE NOUN

   Unemployment has risen by one per cent.

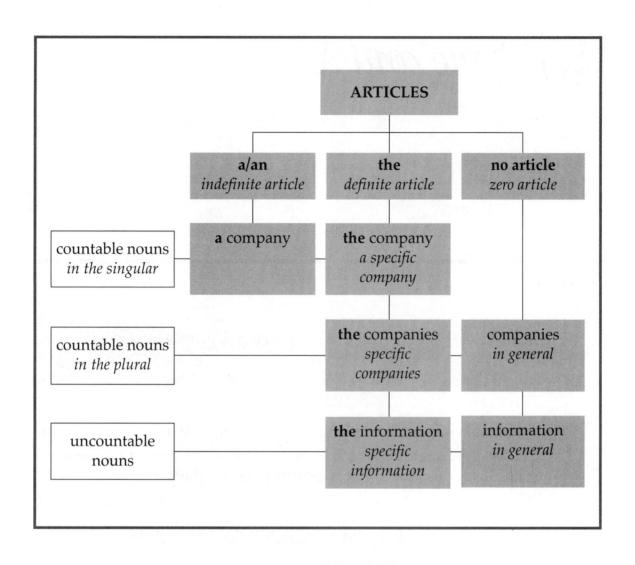

40 Some and Any

Some

> **Some** clauses in the contract will need to be changed before we can agree to it.

With countable nouns in the plural (positive statements)

We have received **some** applications for the vacant post, but not very many.
Some employees also contribute to private pension schemes.

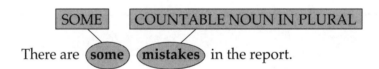
There are **some** **mistakes** in the report.

With uncountable nouns (positive statements)

I'd like **some** information about your products, please.
There's **some** coffee in the pot if you'd like **some**.

I've got **some** good **news** for you.

In questions, especially offers (countable and uncountable nouns)

Would you like **some** tea?
How about **some** cake?
Would you like **some** biscuits?

In other questions, often when we expect the answer 'yes' (countable and uncountable nouns)

Could you give me **some** information about trains to London, please?
Could you give me **some** advice about these software packages?
Could you give me **some** coins in exchange for this note, please?

Any

> I wrote to the company last month asking for advice, but I haven't received **any** reply yet.

In questions with countable nouns in the plural

Are there **any** letters for me in the post?
Have you got **any** cigarettes?

In negative statements with countable nouns in the plural

He can't speak **any** foreign languages.
There aren't **any** delegates from Finland at the conference.

In questions with uncountable nouns

Will this cause you **any** trouble?
Have you got **any** time for a meeting next Monday?

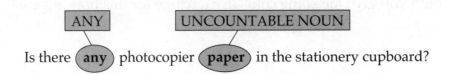

Is there **any** photocopier **paper** in the stationery cupboard?

In negative statements with uncountable nouns

I haven't got **any** money with me.
There isn't **any** milk in the fridge.

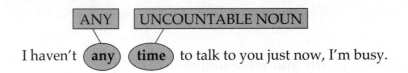

I haven't **any** **time** to talk to you just now, I'm busy.

In positive statements

Let's meet on Tuesday. **Any** time is all right for me.
(*Meaning: I don't mind which time.*)

I'll be pleased to answer **any** questions you may have.
(*Meaning: **all** your questions.*)

Any good manager will tell you that quality is of the utmost importance.
(*Meaning: **all** managers will tell you that.*)

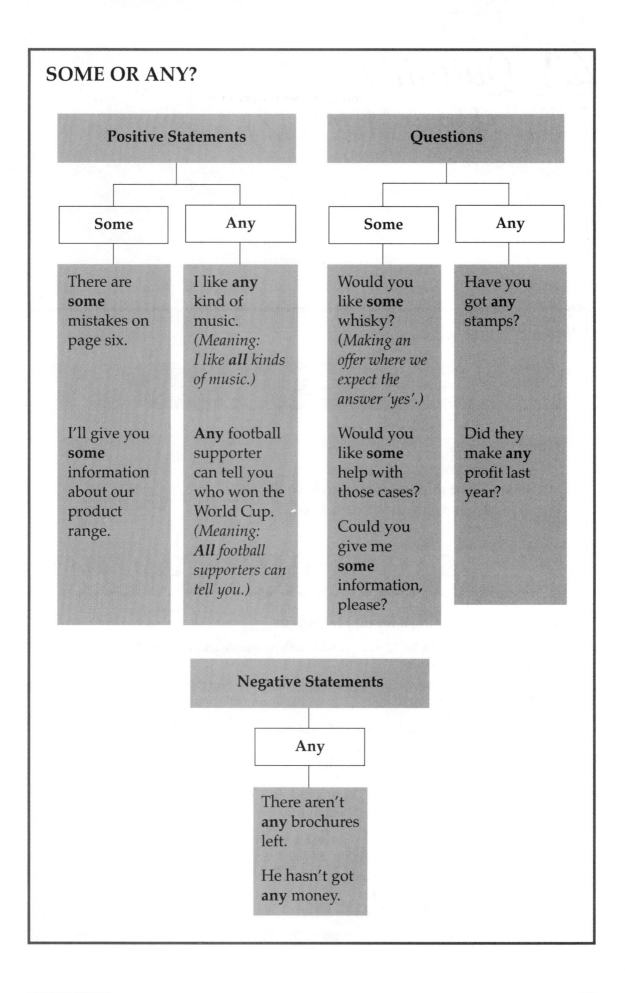

41 Quantity (How Much...?)

A lot/a lot of

> Have you got **a lot of** work to do?

Other examples

I have **a lot of** questions to ask you.
We have **a lot of** sales representatives in the UK.
It cost **a lot** to have the printer repaired.

Using a lot of/a lot/lots of

1. '**A lot of**' is used with both countable and uncountable nouns:

   a lot of components   (countable noun)
   a lot of time   (uncountable noun)

2. '**A lot**' is used without a noun:

   He earns **a lot**.
   I use my mobile phone **a lot**.

3. '**Lots of**' is more informal than '**a lot of**':

   Lots of British people drink tea.

4. '**A lot/a lot of/lots of**' are used in positive statements and sometimes in questions and negative statements:

   Lots of the materials we use are recycled.
   Are there **a lot of** restaurants in that area?
   He doesn't earn **a lot** (**of** money).

Much

> How **much** time have we got before the meeting starts?

Other examples
How **much** do you charge for your services?
Do you have **much** contact with the Berlin office?
Dr. Lehmann doesn't speak **much** English so we'll need an interpreter.
I won't be leaving the office till late. I've got so **much** work to do.

Note
*'Much' is used with **uncountable nouns**. It is used very often in questions and negative statements.*

How **much money** does he earn?
There isn't **much paper** left.

It is sometimes used in positive statements:
Much of the work has already been completed.

*We do not often use **'much'** followed immediately by a noun in positive statements in spoken English. Instead, we use **'a lot of'**.*

❗ Typical Errors	Correct
~~He's got much money.~~	He's got **a lot of** money.

DETERMINERS

Many

> There weren't **many** questions at the end of the presentation.

Other examples

How **many** employees are there in your department?
How **many** languages do you speak?
I have some clients in the south of England, but not **many**.
Many of our competitors went out of business during the recession.
There aren't **many** products of this type on the market.
There weren't as **many** people as expected at the Trade Fair.

Note

*'Many' is used with **countable nouns**. It is used very often in questions and negative statements.*

Did you take **many photographs** when you were on holiday?
There aren't **many items** on the agenda today.

It is sometimes used in positive statements:

Many of our employees speak at least one foreign language.

We do not often use 'many' followed immediately by a noun in positive statements in spoken English. Instead, we use 'a lot of'.

❗ Typical Errors	Correct
~~There were many people at the conference.~~	There were **a lot of** people at the conference.

A few/few

There were only **a few** cars on the road so we got here quickly.

Other examples

The new product will be available on the market in **a few** months' time.
I've been to Moscow **a few** times.
I'll ask him to call you back in **a few** minutes.
Very **few** people showed any interest in the idea.
Only **a few** people attended the conference.
I spoke to the branch manager **a few** days ago.
Few tourists visit this area in the winter.

Using a few/few

A few

'A few' is used with countable nouns.

We have **a few** customers in Japan.

He only smokes **a few cigarettes** a day.
(**'A few'** means a **small number** [not many].)

'A few' has a positive meaning:
I'll see you again in **a few** weeks' time

It is often used with **'only'** which makes it more negative:
There were **only a few** interesting books on the shelves.

Few

'Few' is used with **countable nouns** to talk about **a smaller number than expected**:

Few people support this initiative.
(We expected more people to support it.)

They made **few** mistakes.
(I expected them to make more mistakes.)
They made **a few** mistakes.
(They made **some** mistakes, but not many.)

DETERMINERS

A little/little

There is only **a little** money left in the Petty Cash box.

Other examples

He has **little** interest in the job.
He can speak only **a little** Arabic.
We have only **a little** time left so let's try and come to a decision.
I need **a little** more time to consider your proposal.
We've made **little** progress with our research so far.

Using a little/little

A little

'A little' is used with uncountable nouns:

I'd like **a little** more **time** to think about this.

"Would you like some more **wine**?"
"Just **a little**, please."

'A little' means **a small amount** (not much). It is often used with **'only'**:

I have **only a little** free time.

Little

'Little' without **'a'** emphasises **how small the amount is**:

There was **little** he could do about it.

I have **little** money.
(I don't have as much as I would like.)

I have **a little** money.
(I have some money but not much.)

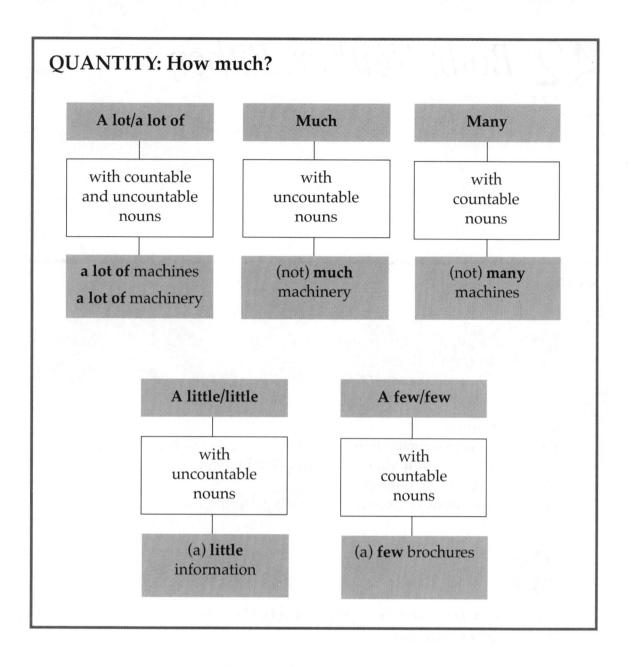

42 Both, Neither, Either

Both

> Peter came up with two interesting ideas at the meeting. **Both** of them are worth considering.

Other examples
We are looking for somewhere in England to locate our branch office, and have considered **both** Manchester and Birmingham.
He has two children, **both** girls.
We have two subsidiary companies. **Both** performed well last year.

'Both' is used to talk about **two** people, objects, ideas, etc.
'Both' takes a **plural verb**.

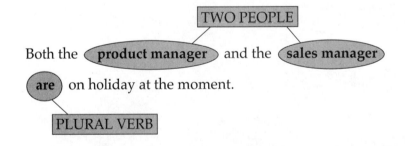

'Both' can also be used at the end of a statement:
He suggested two solutions. We'll try them **both** (or we'll try **both** of them).

Both of...

We use **'both of'** with **'us'**, **'you'**, and **'them'**:
Both of them live in London.

We can also say:
"They **both** live in London", or
"**Both** my brothers live in London."

Neither

I interviewed two people for the vacant post but **neither** candidate was suitable.

Neither (+ singular noun)

The staff are not in favour of this idea and **neither** is management.
Neither machine is expensive.

*We use **'neither'** to talk about two people, objects, ideas, etc.*
'Neither' = not either.
'Neither' takes a singular verb.

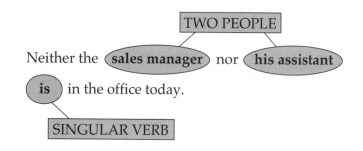

DETERMINERS

Neither...nor

I tried to phone Colin Ford yesterday, but **neither** he **nor** his assistant was in.
Neither Mario **nor** Andrea lives in Rome.

Neither of...

Neither of the estimates is acceptable.
Neither of those two hotels would be suitable for the conference.
I looked at two new computers yesterday but **neither of** them is what I want.
I showed Jane's design to two of my colleagues but **neither of** them liked it.

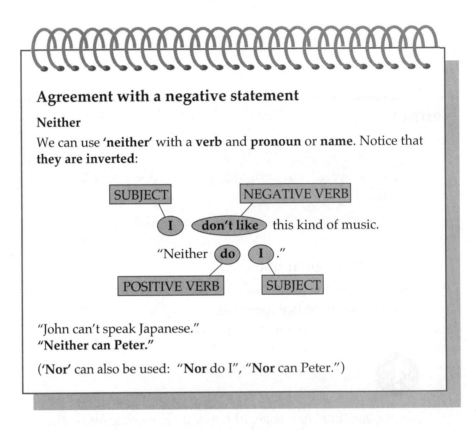

Agreement with a negative statement

Neither

We can use **'neither'** with a **verb** and **pronoun** or **name**. Notice that **they are inverted**:

"John can't speak Japanese."
"**Neither can Peter.**"

('**Nor**' can also be used: "**Nor** do I", "**Nor** can Peter.")

Either

I was invited to two sales promotions last week, but I was so busy I couldn't attend **either**.

Either (one or the other of two people, objects, ideas, etc.)

"Which hotel shall I book you into? The Grand or The Palace?"
"**Either**. I don't mind which."

Either...or

We could meet on **either** Monday **or** Tuesday. Which day would suit you better?

I think **either** you **or** Margaret should go and see Jean-Luc at the Paris office as soon as possible.

I don't have time to see them **either** today **or** tomorrow. I'm fully booked until the beginning of next week.

Can you book me on a flight to Frankfurt? **Either** the ten o'clock, **or** the eleven-thirty.

Either of

I didn't manage to speak to **either of** the candidates yesterday. They were interviewed by our head of department.

Can **either of** you translate this letter for me?

Agreement with a negative statement

Either

Both **'neither'** and **'either'** are used to show agreement with negative statements:

"I don't like this kind of music."
"I don't either." (This is the same meaning as **"Neither do I"**.)

"John can't speak Japanese."
"Alan can't either."
("Neither can Alan.")

"She's not interested in football."
"Neither am I." or **"I'm not either."**

DETERMINERS

43 Each and Every

Each

> Please look at **each** photograph very carefully.

Other examples
Each of the products in the range has different packaging.
Each member of the team is responsible for a different area of the business.
We recruit about twenty new trainees **each** year.
There is a separate brochure for **each** of the services we provide.

'**Each**' is used with countable nouns in the singular:

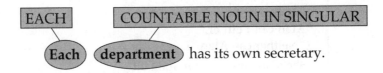

Note
'**Each**' can be used without a noun.
There are four different designs. **Each** is different.
(We can say "**Each one** is different."
We can also say "**Each of them** is different.")

186 GRAMMAR

Every

> We have a brief, informal meeting **every** morning.

Other examples

Elizabeth visits the Berlin office **every** month.

The Personnel Manager gives **every** employee an appraisal at the end of the year.

I'm sorry there aren't any free offices at the moment. **Every** room is being used.

'Every' is used with countable nouns in the singular:

He makes a success of (every) (project) in which he's involved.

Each and every: contrast

Each

We use **'each'** when we talk about people or things separately.

'Each' = ● + ● + ● + ●

Each section in the department has a manager.

Every

We use **'every'** when we talk about people or things as a group:

'Every' = ●●●●●

Every member receives a copy of the society's monthly magazine.
(Meaning: **All** the members receive a copy.)

DETERMINERS

44 Make or Do?

Make

> The directors are going to **make** a **decision** soon about buying a new office building.

Other examples

I'd like to **make** some **changes** to the design.

I've **made** an **appointment** to see the Managing Director at Masons tomorrow.

He **made** a lot of **money** and retired early.

We **made** them an **offer** which they couldn't refuse.

We have **made** a lot of **progress** with the research project.

The company **made** a large **profit** last year.

The company **made** a **loss** on its contract to supply equipment to the government.

One of our customers has **made** a **complaint** about the delay in dealing with her order.

A lot of our employees were **made redundant** during the recession.

Note

'Make' is often used when we are giving the idea of production or creation:
make plans
make alterations

Have you **made** any **plans** for your summer holiday?

Do

> I was interrupted a lot yesterday. I didn't manage to **do** much **work**.

Other examples

"What do you **do for a living**?"
"I'm an electronics engineer."

My company **does** a lot of **business** in the Far East.
Could you **do** me a **favour**? Could you post this letter for me, please?
We have **done** a lot of **research** into consumer attitudes.

Note

'Do' is used to talk about work:

I've got a lot of **work** to **do**.
My son hates **doing** his **homework**.

'Do' is also used in a general way when we do not say what the activity is:

We've got a big problem with this machine. I don't know what to **do** about it.

"What are you **doing** on Saturday?"
"Oh, I'm not **doing** anything special."

Useful words with:

MAKE	DO
an appointment	business
a business trip	the cleaning
changes/alterations	the cooking
a complaint/an apology	exercises
a decision	the housework
a loss	a job/something for a living
a mistake	the shopping
money	someone a favour
a noise	work
an offer	
plans/arrangements	
a profit	
progress	
someone redundant	
a telephone call	

EASILY CONFUSED WORDS

45 Rise or Raise?

Rise

> The level of unemployment always **rises** during a recession.

Other examples

Profits **rose** by five per cent last year.
The sun **rises** in the east.
The demand for this type of product is **rising** all the time.
The cost of raw material **has risen** in the last six months.

Raise

> The government will probably **raise** the tax on petrol next spring.

Other examples

We **raised** our prices last year.
I'm sorry I can't hear you. Could you **raise** your voice a little?
The government may have to **raise** interest rates in the next few months.
We continued with the meeting since nobody **raised** any objections.
They **raised** most of the money from private investors.

'Raise' *must be followed by an object:*

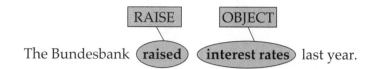

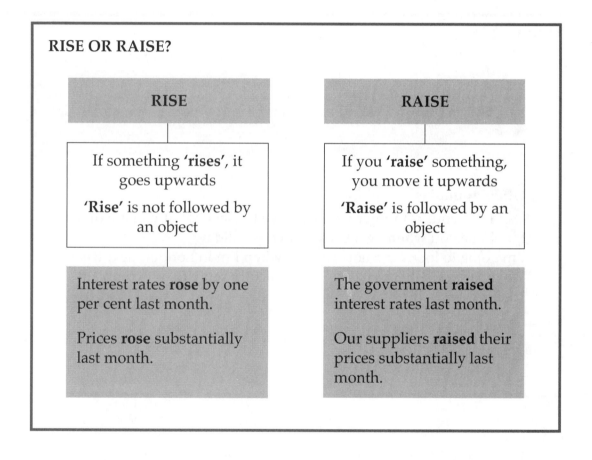

RISE OR RAISE?

RISE

If something **'rises'**, it goes upwards

'Rise' is not followed by an object

Interest rates **rose** by one per cent last month.

Prices **rose** substantially last month.

RAISE

If you **'raise'** something, you move it upwards

'Raise' is followed by an object

The government **raised** interest rates last month.

Our suppliers **raised** their prices substantially last month.

46 When or If?

When

> "**When** will you give him the letter?"
> "I'll give it to him **when** I see him tomorrow. He's coming here for a meeting."

Other examples

Can I use your computer **when** you've finished what you are doing?
I'll phone you **when** I get back from my holiday.
I'm going to look for a new camera **when** I'm in London next week.
We'll pay you **when** you give a satisfactory reply to our complaint, not before.

If

> We're going out for a drink this evening. **If** you're free, you're welcome to join us.

Other examples

If he gets the job he's applied for, he'll have to move house.

"Could you give Mr. Dodd the message, please?"
"I don't know whether I'll be seeing him. I'll certainly tell him **if** I do."

"What would you do **if** you won the lottery?"
"**If** I won, I'd probably buy a new car."

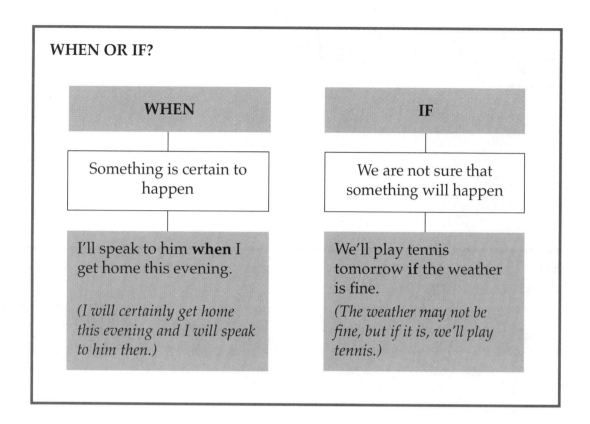

！ Typical Error	Correct
~~I'll let you know when the Board agree to the proposal.~~	I'll let you know **if** the Board agree to the proposal.

See also *Conditionals: Introduction* (Unit 13).

47 So or Such?

So

> The estimates we received were **so** high that we decided to invite other firms to submit tenders for the work.

Other examples

He drives **so** carelessly. I'm sure he'll have an accident before long!
The weather was **so** bad at the weekend that we decided to stay at home.
I've got **so** much to do, I'll have to work late tonight.
Profits were **so** good last year that we decided to give all staff a large bonus.
Both new employees are **so** efficient. We are really pleased with their work.

So...that

'So...that' is used to show a result:
The car was **so** expensive **that** I couldn't buy it.

Such

> It was **such** a good training course that we were sorry when it came to an end.

Other examples

It is **such** an old and slow computer that we should really consider buying a new one.

It was **such** an interesting film that I decided to buy the book.

It's **such** a long time since I've seen her.

Such a high quality product is bound to be expensive.

Such...that

'**Such...that**' is used to show a result:

It was **such** an expensive car **that** I couldn't buy it.

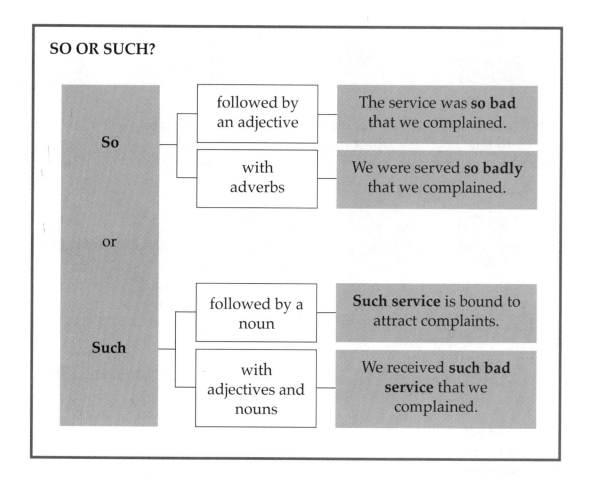

EASILY CONFUSED WORDS

48 Time

Telling the time

"What time is it, please?"
"It's **half past ten**."

It's twenty-five to ten
It's nine thirty-five

It's (a) quarter past three
It's three fifteen

It's twenty-five past nine
It's nine twenty-five

It's (a) quarter to eight
It's seven forty-five

It's ten to twelve
It's eleven fifty

It's one o'clock
It's one

It's ten past six
It's six ten

It's half past five
It's five thirty

It's five to three
It's two fifty-five

It's twenty past seven
It's seven twenty

It's four minutes past two

It's twelve minutes to three

It's five past four

It's twenty to eleven
It's ten forty

GRAMMAR

The twenty-four hour clock

"What time does the train leave?"
"It leaves at **twenty fifteen**."

20:15

10:00	**22:00**	**9:05**	**3:10**	**13:15**
ten	twenty-two hundred hours	nine-o-five	three ten	thirteen fifteen
(ten o'clock)	*(ten o'clock)*	*(five past nine)*	*(ten past three)*	*(quarter past one)*
14:20	**20:25**	**16:30**		**15:35**
fourteen twenty	twenty twenty-five	sixteen thirty		fifteen thirty-five
(twenty past two)	*(eight twenty-five)*	*(four thirty)*		*(three thirty-five)*
18:40	**19:45**	**21:50**		**16:55**
eighteen forty	nineteen forty-five	twenty-one fifty		sixteen fifty-five
(six forty, twenty to seven)	*(seven forty-five, quarter to eight)*	*(nine fifty, ten to ten)*		*(four fifty-five, five to four)*

The twenty-four hour clock is used for timetables, schedules and official meetings.

Talking about time

For the full hour, it is usual, in spoken English, to say **'ten'**, rather than **'twenty-two hundred'** or **'twenty-two hundred hours'**.

We sometimes use **'am'** and **'pm'** when talking about time:
The meeting is at 9am. (9 in the morning.)
We usually have dinner at 7.30pm. (7.30 in the evening.)

49 The Diary

DAYS	MONTHS		SEASONS
Monday	January	July	spring
Tuesday	February	August	summer
Wednesday	March	September	autumn
Thursday	April	October	winter
Friday	May	November	
Saturday	June	December	
Sunday			

DATES

1st	first	13th	thirteenth
2nd	second	14th	fourteenth
3rd	third	15th	fifteenth
4th	fourth	16th	sixteenth
5th	fifth	17th	seventeenth
6th	sixth	18th	eighteenth
7th	seventh	19th	nineteenth
8th	eighth	20th	twentieth
9th	ninth	21st	twenty-first
10th	tenth	22nd	twenty-second
11th	eleventh	30th	thirtieth
12th	twelfth	31st	thirty-first

We say *'December the twenty-fifth'*, or *'the twenty-fifth of December'*, but we write *'25 December'*, *'December 25'*, or *'December 25th'*.

 December twenty-five.

YEARS

1800	Eighteen hundred
1990	Nineteen-ninety
1995	Nineteen-ninety-five
2000	Two thousand
2006	Two thousand and six

PERIODS OF TIME

10 years = a decade
25 years = a quarter of a century
50 years = half a century
100 years = a century

We say 'in the 18th century'.

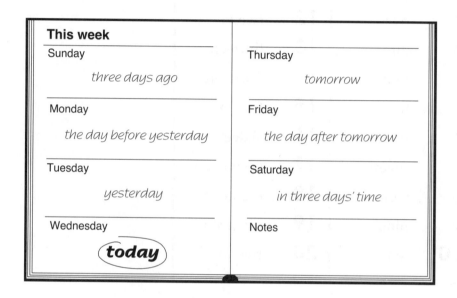

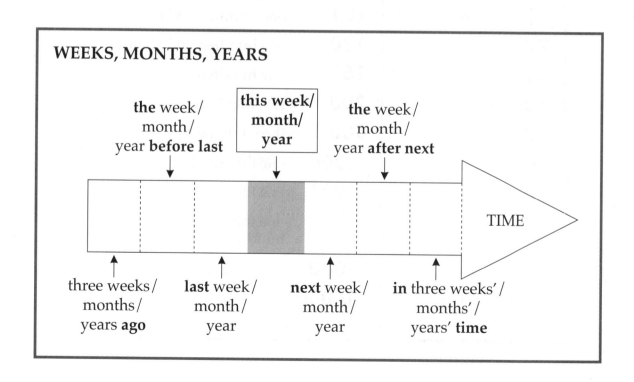

GENERAL INFORMATION

50 Numbers

1	one	11	eleven
2	two	12	twelve
3	three	13	thirteen
4	four	14	fourteen
5	five	15	fifteen
6	six	16	sixteen
7	seven	17	seventeen
8	eight	18	eighteen
9	nine	19	nineteen
10	ten	20	twenty

21	twenty-one	101	one hundred and one
22	twenty-two	120	one hundred and twenty
30	thirty	151	one hundred and fifty-one
40	forty	200	two hundred
50	fifty	300	three hundred
60	sixty	1,000	one thousand
70	seventy	1,001	one thousand and one
80	eighty	1,562	one thousand, five hundred and sixty-two
90	ninety	2,000	two thousand
100	one hundred	10,000	ten thousand

NUMBERS

We write	We say
235	two hundred and thirty-five
6,781	six thousand, seven hundred and eighty-one
24,500	twenty four thousand, five hundred
600,000	six hundred thousand
8,238,000	eight million, two hundred and thirty-eight thousand

MATHEMATICAL SYMBOLS

We write	We say
=	equals
+	plus
−	minus
×	multiplied by *(times)*
÷	divided by
6 + 7 = 13	six plus seven equals thirteen
100 − 20	one hundred minus twenty
24 × 15	twenty-four times *(multiplied by)* fifteen
60 ÷ 3	sixty divided by three

DECIMALS

We write	We say
0.5	point five *(nought point five)*
1.05	one point 'o' five
2.75	two point seven five

*In English, decimals are shown with a point '·' **not** a comma ','.*

PRICES

We write	We say
£3.50	three pounds fifty (pence)
£75	seventy-five pounds
$2.75	two dollars seventy-five (cents)
$40,000	forty thousand dollars

FRACTIONS

We write	We say
$1/3$	a third *(one third)*
$2/3$	two thirds
$1/4$	a quarter
$3/4$	three quarters
$1/2$	a half
$1/5$	a fifth *(one fifth)*
$3/8$	three eighths
$1/16$	one sixteenth

PERCENTAGES

We write	We say
2%	two per cent
50%	fifty per cent
75%	seventy-five per cent

GRAMMAR

GENERAL INFORMATION

51 British and American Grammar Differences

Past Simple and Present Perfect

Americans use the **Past Simple** for talking about new and recent information, particularly when **'just'**, **'already'**, and **'yet'** are used. In these cases, British English uses the **Present Perfect**.

They **have** just **opened** a new factory.	They just **opened** a new factory.
I'm afraid he isn't in the office. He**'s gone** out.	I'm afraid he isn't in the office. He **went** out.
I**'ve** already **had** dinner.	I already **had** dinner.
Have you **finished** that project yet?	**Did** you **finish** that project yet?
Have you ever **been** to Paris?	**Did** you **ever** go to Paris?

Prepositions

in the team **in** Surrey Street **at** the weekend	**on** the team **on** Surrey Street **on** the weekend

I **wrote to** the authorities.	I **wrote** the authorities.

We **are meeting** the authorities next week. I'll **talk to** him tomorrow.	We **are meeting with** the authorities next week. I'll **talk with** him tomorrow.

It's a quarter **to** four.	It's a quarter **of** four.

52 Common Problems

Certain aspects of grammar cause problems for many learners of different nationalities. Listed below are some common mistakes and a corrected version. It is a good idea to keep a checklist of your own common mistakes with a corrected version.

Verbs: tenses

Typical mistakes **Correct**

~~I'm living in London and I'm working for Lloyds.~~

I **live** in London and I **work** for Lloyds.

See Units 1 & 2, *Present Simple/Present Continuous*.

~~The UK is operating a compulsory system of social security.~~

The UK **operates** a compulsory system of social security.

See Units 1 & 2, *Present Simple/Present Continuous*.

~~I am working for Siemens since six years.~~

I **have worked/have been working** for Siemens **for** six years.

See Units 6 & 7, *Present Perfect/Present Perfect Continuous*.

~~Charles has been in London last week.~~

Charles **was** in London last week.

See Units 3 & 6, *Past Simple/Present Perfect*.

Typical mistakes	Correct
~~I will play tennis with Bob on Saturday afternoon.~~	**I'm playing/going to play** tennis with Bob on Saturday afternoon.

See Units 2 & 10, *Present Continuous/Going to*.

Verbs: Conditionals

Typical mistakes	Correct
~~If a company will have its headquarters in Germany, it is subject to German tax.~~	If a company **has** its headquarters in Germany, it is subject to German tax.

See Unit 14, *Conditional 0*.

Typical mistakes	Correct
~~If you will relocate the factory, the overheads will be lower.~~	If you **relocate** the factory, the overheads will be lower.

See Unit 15, *Conditional 1*.

Typical mistakes	Correct
~~If he would have driven more carefully, he wouldn't have had an accident.~~	If he **had driven** more carefully, he wouldn't have had an accident.

See Unit 17, *Conditional 3*.

Verbs: Gerund

Typical mistakes	Correct
~~We look forward to hear from you soon.~~	We look forward to **hearing** from you soon.

See Unit 19, *Gerund*.

Typical mistakes	Correct
~~After to calculate the figures, he wrote the letter.~~	After **calculating** the figures, he wrote the letter.

See Unit 19, *Gerund*.

GENERAL INFORMATION

Verbs: Modals

Typical mistakes

~~We don't must be late for the meeting.~~

Correct

We **mustn't** be late for the meeting.

See Unit 26, *Modal Verbs*.

Adjectives and adverbs

Typical mistakes

~~He speaks English very good.~~

~~He speaks very well English.~~

Correct

He speaks English very **well**.

He speaks English very **well**.

See Unit 28, *Adjectives and Adverbs*.

~~The normally procedure is to approach the authorities first.~~

The **normal** procedure is to approach the authorities first.

See Unit 28, *Adjectives and Adverbs*.

~~It is a high sophisticated product.~~

It is a **highly** sophisticated product.

See Unit 28, *Adjectives and Adverbs*.

~~The new machine is more better as the old one.~~

The new machine is **much** better **than** the old one.

See Unit 30, *Comparatives*.

Relative clauses

Typical mistakes

~~The manager which implemented the new staff contracts was Harold Smith.~~

Correct

The manager **who** implemented the new staff contracts was Harold Smith.

See Unit 33, *Relative Causes*.

Countable and uncountable nouns

Typical mistakes

~~Could you give me some informations about this?~~

Correct

Could you give me some **information** about this?

See Unit 38, *Countable and Uncountable Nouns*.

~~How much people were at the meeting?~~

How **many** people were at the meeting?

See Unit 41, *Quantity*.

GENERAL INFORMATION

CHECKLIST

Use this checklist to note examples of mistakes you often make, together with the correct version.

Mistakes I often make	Correct

CHECKLIST

Use this checklist to note examples of mistakes you often make, together with the correct version.

Mistakes I often make	Correct

CHECKLIST

Use this checklist to note examples of mistakes you often make, together with the correct version.

Mistakes I often make	Correct

CHECKLIST

Use this checklist to note examples of mistakes you often make, together with the correct version.

Mistakes I often make	Correct

CHECKLIST

Use this checklist to note examples of mistakes you often make, together with the correct version.

Mistakes I often make	Correct

Everyday Communication

53 Greetings and Farewells

Greetings

- **Good morning**, Mr. Jackson.

▼ **Good morning. How are you?**

- **Very well, thank you. And you?**

▼ **I'm fine, thank you.** It's a long time since I've seen you.

- Yes, I've been to Italy, on holiday.

▼ Did you have a good time?

- Yes, the weather was wonderful.

Good morning. How are you?   Very well, thank you. And you?

I'm fine, thank you

EVERYDAY COMMUNICATION

- **Hello**, John. **Nice to see you**. How are you?
- Hello, Mike. I'm fine, thanks. How are you?
- Very well, thanks. I'm glad I've seen you. I was going to ring you.
- Were you? What about?
- Well, I wanted to talk to you about the Sports Club meeting next week.

Hello... Nice to see you

- **Hi** Tina!
- Hello, Jane. **How are things?**
- **Not too bad. How about you?**
- **Fine, thanks.** Have you got time for a coffee?
- Yes, I'd love one.

Hi!	How are things?
Not too bad. How about you?	Fine, thanks

'Hi!' is used in:

Informal British English

American English

EVERYDAY COMMUNICATION

Farewells

- It was a very useful meeting. I'll send you a letter confirming the details of what we've agreed today.

▼ Good.

- You ought to receive it some time next week. Will that be all right?

▼ Yes. That's fine.

- Well, thank you. **It was nice to see you again. I hope you'll have a good journey** back to Madrid.

▼ Thank you. **Goodbye**, Mr. Sims. **I look forward to seeing you again** next month.

- Yes, so do I. **Goodbye**.

It was nice to see you again It was nice meeting you *(first time of meeting)*	I hope you'll have a good journey
Goodbye	I look forward to seeing you again

- Thanks very much for the coffee, Mary.
▼ **It was nice to see you. See you again soon, I hope.**
- Yes, I'll phone you to arrange a lunch, perhaps. **Bye!**
▼ **Cheerio!**

It was nice to see you	See you again soon, I hope
Bye!	Cheerio!

GREETINGS AND FAREWELLS

GREETINGS

Hello
Hi!

Good morning
Good afternoon
Good evening

FAREWELLS

Bye!
Cheerio!

Goodbye
Goodnight

See you again soon
I look forward to seeing you again soon
It was nice meeting you

'Good evening' is a *greeting* that might be used after about five or six o'clock in the evening, until quite late.

'Goodnight' is a *farewell* that might be used after it has got dark in the evening.

EVERYDAY COMMUNICATION

54 Introductions

Introducing yourself

(Informal meeting/at a party)

- **Hello!** May I join you?
- ▼ Yes, please do.
- **My name's** Jim Anderson.
- ▼ **Hi! I'm** Georgina Smith. Where are you from?
- Scotland originally, but I live in London now. How about you?
- ▼ I'm from Birmingham.

Hello!	Hi!
I'm...	My name's...

(At a conference)

- ● Good morning. **May I introduce myself?** My name's Susan Holmes. I'm in the sales department at Bensons.
- ▼ **How do you do?** I'm Arnold Jones. I work for Ashley Electronics as a Regional Sales Manager.
- ● **How do you do? Pleased to meet you.**

May I introduce myself?	How do you do?
How do you do?	Pleased to meet you

'Hi!' is used in:

Informal British English   *American English*

Introducing other people

(At a party)

- ● Jane, **this is** Bob. He's an old friend from University. Bob, Jane.
- ▼ **Hello**, Bob. **Nice to meet you**.
- ■ **Hi,** Jane. I've heard a lot about you.

This is...	Hello/Hi! Nice to meet you

EVERYDAY COMMUNICATION

(Formal/at a business meeting)

● Mrs. Diaz, **may I introduce** Paolo Conti from Fiat? Mr. Conti, **this is** Sophia Diaz from our sales division.

▼ How do you do?

■ How do you do? **Pleased to meet you.**

| May I introduce...? | This is... |

| (I'm) pleased to meet you |

We often say *'How do you do?'* when we meet someone for the first time. This is not a real question and the answer is exactly the same: *'How do you do?'*

'How do you do?' is not the same as *'How are you?'*

! Typical Errors	Correct
● ~~"How do you do?"~~	● "How do you do?"
▼ ~~"Very well, thank you."~~	▼ "How do you do?"

Introducing other people
When introducing a man and a woman to each other, it is usual to speak to the woman first. When introducing two men or two women, we usually speak to the older person first.

Shaking hands
British and American people shake hands when they meet someone for the first time. Hand-shaking is not as common as in many other countries. In Britain and America, people do not shake hands when greeting or saying goodbye to colleagues and friends every day. They do shake hands when they meet someone they have not seen for a long time and also at business meetings.

INTRODUCTIONS

INTRODUCING YOURSELF

Person 1	Person 2
Informal	
Hello! My name's... ⇨	Hello! I'm...
Formal	
May I introduce myself? My name's... ⇨	How do you do?
How do you do? I'm *(name)* ⇨	Pleased to meet you

INTRODUCING OTHER PEOPLE

Person 1	Person 2	Person 3
Informal		
Jane this is... ⇨	Hello! Nice to meet you ⇨	Hello!/Hi!
Formal		
May I introduce... This is... ⇨	How do you do? ⇨	How do you do? (I'm) pleased to meet you

EVERYDAY COMMUNICATION

55 Socialising: Polite Phrases

Asking for something (requests)

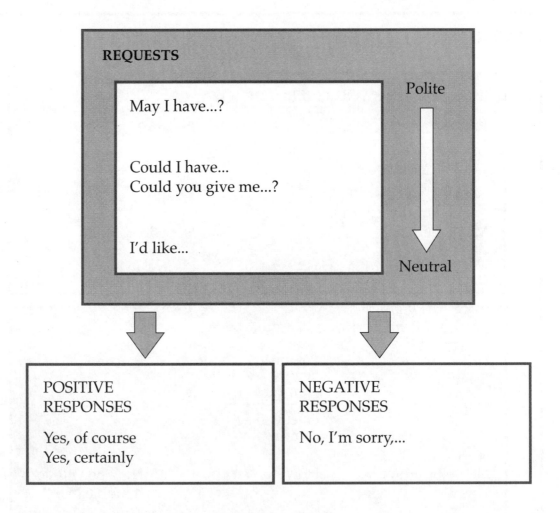

Apologising

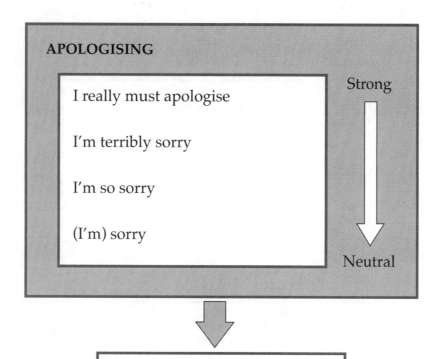

APOLOGISING

I really must apologise

I'm terribly sorry

I'm so sorry

(I'm) sorry

Strong → Neutral

RESPONSES
That's all right
That's quite all right
Don't worry about it
That's perfectly all right

*In British English, **'sorry'** is used **after** you have done something. **'Excuse me'** is used **before** you do something, for example, when you want to interrupt someone during a meeting.*

Excuse me, could I come in here?

*In American English, **'excuse me'** is often used instead of **'sorry'**.*

EVERYDAY COMMUNICATION

Asking for permission

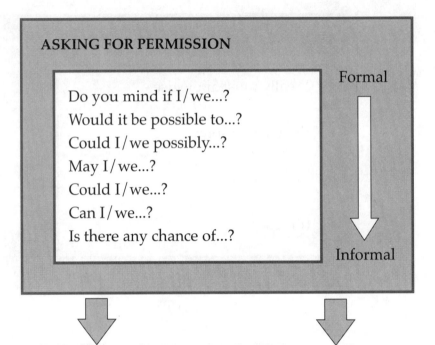

ASKING FOR PERMISSION

Do you mind if I/we...?
Would it be possible to...?
Could I/we possibly...?
May I/we...?
Could I/we...?
Can I/we...?
Is there any chance of...?

Formal → Informal

GIVING PERMISSION

Yes, of course
Yes, certainly
By all means
Yes, that will be all right
Sure

Not at all. Go ahead
(*in answer to* **'Do you/Would you mind...?'**)

REFUSING PERMISSION

I'm afraid not
I'm sorry

Well, I'd rather you didn't
(*in answer to* **'Do you mind...?'**)

"Do you/Would you mind...?" *means* "Is it a problem for you?"
A **positive** *answer is therefore,* "Not at all. Go ahead".
A **negative** (but polite) *answer is* "Well, I'd rather you didn't".

EVERYDAY COMMUNICATION

Asking someone to do something

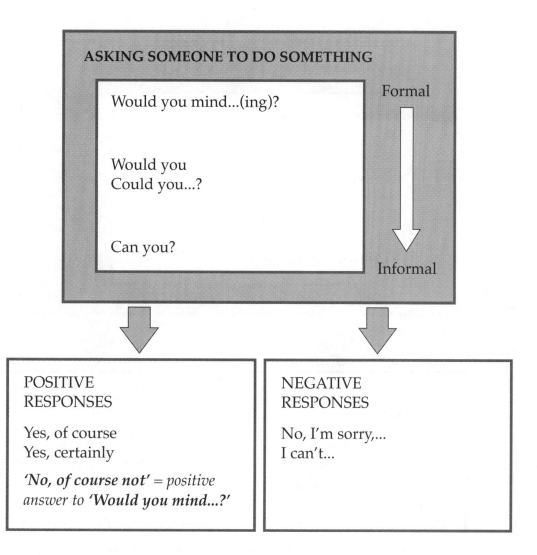

"Would you mind...?" means *"Would it be a problem for you (to do something)?"*
A **positive** answer is, therefore, *"No, of course not."*

Inviting

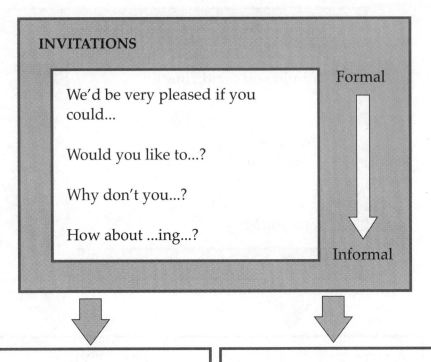

Offers: making offers to help

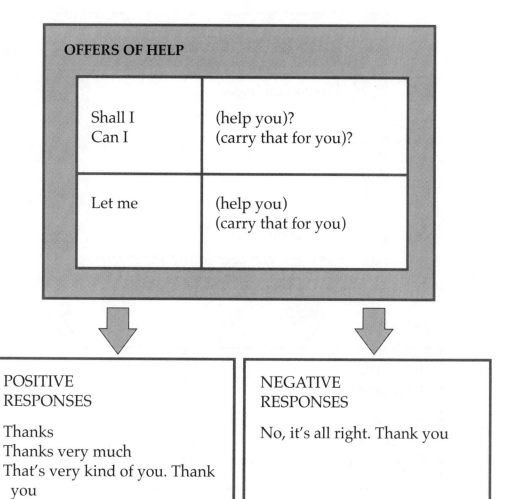

Offering something (some coffee, a cigarette, etc.)

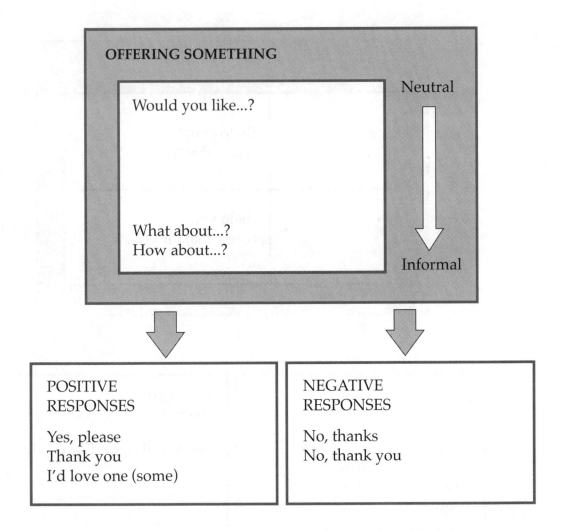

*In English **'thank you'** (without **'yes'**, or **'no'**) is a positive answer, meaning "Yes, please."*

Thanking

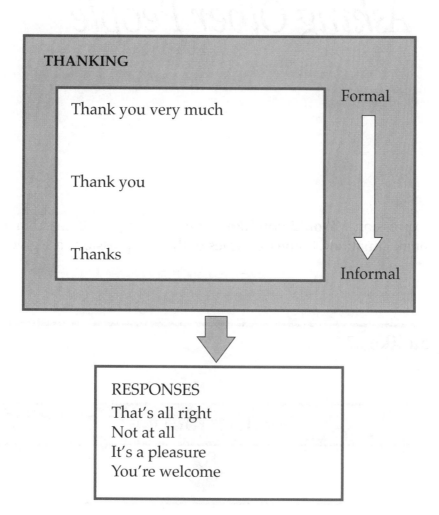

*To make **'thanks'** stronger, we sometimes add "It's very kind of you" or "I do appreciate it" (formal).*

56 Socialising: Asking Other People

Some expressions, **'Would you like...'**, for example, can be used in a variety of different situations. Some examples of these expressions are given here.

Would you like...?

WOULD YOU LIKE

something to eat/drink/a cigarette?
some help with that luggage?
to come to a football match on Saturday?
a copy of the sales report?

"Would you like" is used for both offers, *"Would you like a cup of coffee?"* and invitations, *"Would you like to have dinner with us on Sunday evening?"*

EVERYDAY COMMUNICATION

I'd like...

'**I'd like**' is used when you ask someone for something.

I'D LIKE

a pint of lager / two coffees, please.
to speak to Mr. Jones, please.
to use your telephone if I may.
to go to the conference in Stockholm.
to book a single room for Friday please.

Could/may I have

'**Could/may I have...**' is used when you ask for something.

COULD/MAY I HAVE

a newspaper in the morning, please?
two pints of beer, please?
a day off tomorrow?
your report by Friday?

EVERYDAY COMMUNICATION

Would you mind...ing?

'Would you mind...ing? is used when you ask another person to do something for you.

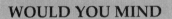

WOULD YOU MIND

shutting the door?
lending me your pen?
helping me with this translation?
not smoking in here?

Do you mind if I...?

'Do you mind' is used when you ask another person if you can do something.

DO YOU MIND

if I smoke?
if I open the window?
if I borrow this book?
if I use your phone?

57 Reacting

Reacting to good news

- Hi, Paul. How are you?
- ▼ Fine. I've just heard that I've got the contract with Jacksons.
- **Congratulations! That's great news.**

| Congratulations! | That's great news |

- How did you get on with your final accountancy exam, Roger?
- ▼ I passed!
- **Well done!** I'm so pleased for you.

| Well done! |

Reacting to bad news

- Hello, Rachel. How are you?
- ▼ I'm fine, but my husband's ill. He's in hospital.
- **Oh, I'm sorry to hear that.**

> I'm sorry to hear that

- Hello, Sam. How is everything?
- ▼ Well, we've just lost an important contract, I'm afraid.
- Oh, **that's terrible news!**

> That's terrible news!

- I'm sorry, Caroline. I can't come out for a drink this evening. I've got to work late. We're so busy at the moment.
- ▼ Oh, **what a shame!** Some other time perhaps.

> What a shame/pity!

EVERYDAY COMMUNICATION

Showing interest

- I've just been reading about the new multimedia computers. We are going to buy some for the company.

▼ **How interesting!**

How interesting!

- Did I tell you that the Sales Manager has been dismissed?
▼ **Really?**

Really?

- So, we decided to start a new branch in Budapest.
▼ **That's very interesting!**

That's very interesting!

REACTING TO GOOD NEWS

- Congratulations!
- That's great news
- Well done!

REACTING TO BAD NEWS

- I'm so sorry to hear that
- That's terrible news
- What a shame/pity!

SHOWING INTEREST

- How interesting!
- Really?
- That's very interesting

EVERYDAY COMMUNICATION

58 Comparing and Contrasting

Comparing

> Our prices, **in comparison with** those of competitors, are **relatively** low.

Other examples

Compared with other similar products, this is of a very high quality.

If you compare prices in Switzerland **with** those in England, you will find that Switzerland is more expensive, on the whole.

There is no comparison between the software we use nowadays **and** that used ten years ago. Modern software packages are much more flexible.

Contrasting

> Profits for the first half of the year were very encouraging **despite** the poor demand in January.

Other examples

Although Paul Jackson is a strong candidate for the post, James Brown fulfills all our criteria.

Even though this brand has been reasonably successful, we have decided to discontinue it and concentrate on improving our leading brands.

We expect positive results in the long-term, **in spite of** poor short-term forecasts.

There are some advantages and disadvantages in setting up a company in Norway. **On the one hand** we have extremely good contacts there, **on the other hand** there are few tax advantages.

This sector of the market has not improved, **whereas** the general trend has been encouraging.

While our service is highly regarded by our clients, it is still necessary to make some improvements.

Note

Compare — To **'compare'** is to examine one thing in relation to another to show similarities and differences.

See also *Comparatives and Superlatives* (Unit 30).

Contrast — To **'contrast'** is to compare things that are dissimilar, especially to show the differences between them.

COMPARING AND CONTRASTING

COMPARING	CONTRASTING
compared with	although
if you compare...with	despite
in comparison with	even though
relatively	in spite of
there is no comparison between...and...	on the one hand,...on the other hand
	whereas
	while

EVERYDAY COMMUNICATION

59 Connecting Ideas

Adding extra points

> The tax allowances are **not only** substantial, they are **also** easy to claim.

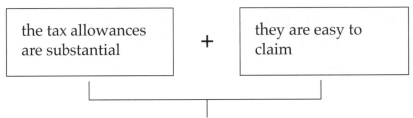

The tax allowances are **not only** substantial,
they are **also** easy to claim.

Other examples

In addition to the factors I have already mentioned, we need to consider the future implications of this deal.

As well as appointing extra staff, we should install some extra computers.

Stating alternatives

> As I see it, **there are two possible options open to us. One is** to take immediate legal action against the suppliers for breach of contract. **Alternatively,** we can give them another chance but warn them that, if things don't improve, we'll have to sue them.

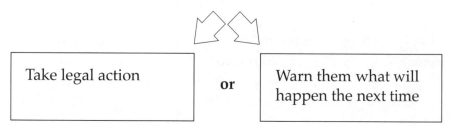

Other examples

We could establish a branch in the Ukraine straightaway. **An alternative would be** to send out representatives from our Moscow operation.

Instead of discussing our domestic market, we should be considering our export trade.

Explanation/clarification

The tax rates are progressive. **In other words,** the percentage withheld increases as the income rises.

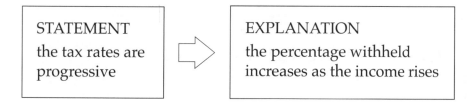

Other examples

I expect to complete my investigation within three weeks, and it will take me two more weeks to write my report. **That is to say,** you should have the report before the end of April.

The company spends five hundred thousand dollars on training each year and employs one thousand staff. **This means that** annual spending on training amounts to five hundred dollars for each member of staff.

Giving examples

> As you can see from the figures, last year was very disappointing for many reasons. **To give an example,** we lost one of our major customers, Rutters, who changed their product range and no longer needed our materials.

Other examples

We try to enter a market by making our products as attractive as possible. We do this by, **for example,** using effective advertising and starting with low-priced products.

There are several advantages in using this type of engine. **For instance,** it is much more economical than the one we've got at the moment.

*All the phrases listed above are more common in **formal presentations** or in **written English** than in informal spoken English.*

CONNECTING IDEAS

ADDING EXTRA POINTS

In addition to...	Not only...also
As well as...	

CONNECTING IDEAS

STATING ALTERNATIVES

There are (two) possible options open to us, one is...	
Alternatively,...	We could...
Instead of...	An alternative would be...

EXPLAINING

| In other words,... | That is to say,... | This means that... |

GIVING EXAMPLES

| To give an example,... | For example,... | For instance,... |

60 Describing Trends

Upward trends

Increased sales led to a **rise** in profits last year.

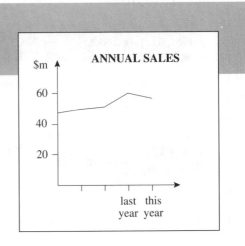

Sales **reached a peak** of sixty million last year

Verbs

Our share of the market **has increased** by three per cent in the last nine months.

The percentage of people who are unemployed in this region **rose** from ten to eleven per cent last year.

In the first quarter of the year, turnover **reached** 11.3 *(eleven point three)* billion dollars.

Our most profitable year so far was 1994 when sales **reached a peak** of sixty million.

Annual production **went up** by 25% *(twenty-five per cent)* between 1990 and 1994.

Sales **climbed** to fifteen million last month which is very encouraging.

Short-term interest rates **rose** during the first half of last year and **peaked** at 8% *(eight per cent)*.

The year started badly but things began **picking up** in March.

Prices **have risen** rapidly in the last month.

Adjectives and nouns

Although monthly demand has fluctuated, the overall trend in the last year has been **upward**.

There has been considerable **growth** in exports to the Far East.

There has been a **boom** in spending since July.

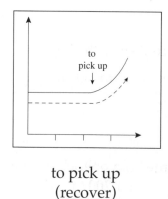

to pick up
(recover)

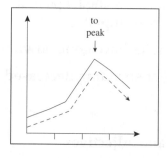

(to reach) a peak
(to peak)

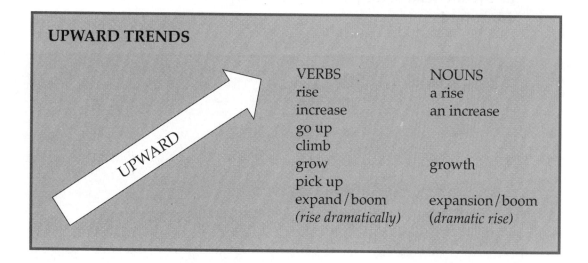

UPWARD TRENDS

UPWARD

VERBS	NOUNS
rise	a rise
increase	an increase
go up	
climb	
grow	growth
pick up	
expand/boom	expansion/boom
(rise dramatically)	*(dramatic rise)*

EVERYDAY COMMUNICATION

Downward trends

Sales **fell** by five per cent last month compared with the previous month.

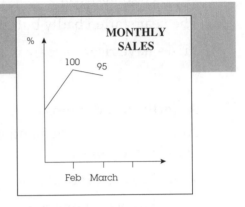

Sales **fell** by five per cent last month

Verbs

The level of unemployment **dropped** last month.

Share prices reached a peak in October and then **slumped**.

Interest rates have **gone down** by one per cent since the beginning of the year.

Consumer spending **decreased** by three per cent in February.

Nouns and adjectives

There was a sharp **fall** in share prices on the Tokyo Stock Exchange yesterday. The Nikkei share index fell by over 1,200 (*one thousand two hundred*) points.

There has been a **decline** in interest in this product recently.

The overall trend in the purchase of our type of products this year has been **downward**.

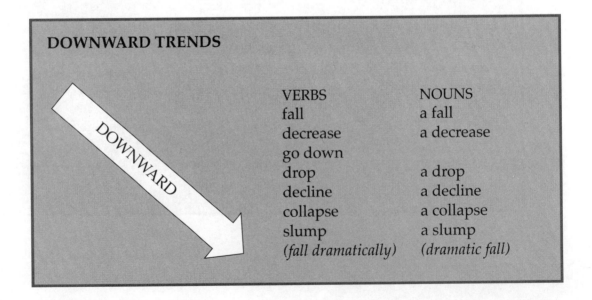

EVERYDAY COMMUNICATION

Stability and fluctuation

> In 1990, our share of the market **stood at** ten per cent. Since then, it has risen steadily and is now nearly twenty per cent.

Other examples

The dollar exchange rate has **fluctuated** by large amounts in the last few months.

Monthly production rose rapidly and then **levelled off** at two thousand units.

Interest rates have **remained stable** since the beginning of the year.

Sales fell throughout the year, but **bottomed out** in January this year. Since then, there has been some improvement.

Note

'Stand at' is used to indicate the level or position of something at a certain time.
In January, sales in this region **stood at** sixty million.

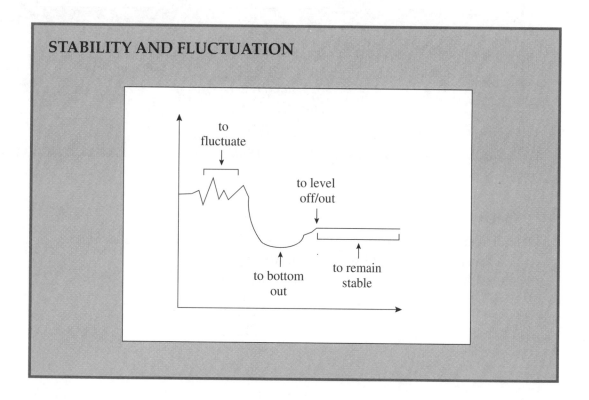

EVERYDAY COMMUNICATION

Degree and speed of changing trends

> There was a **sudden** fall in orders from America which led to a **sharp** decrease in turnover.

Degree

After a **dramatic** fall in demand, we were forced to close down one of our branches.
Prices of raw materials have risen **dramatically** in the last month.
Consumer spending increased **significantly** after the cuts in taxation.
Profits have risen **slightly** in the last six months.

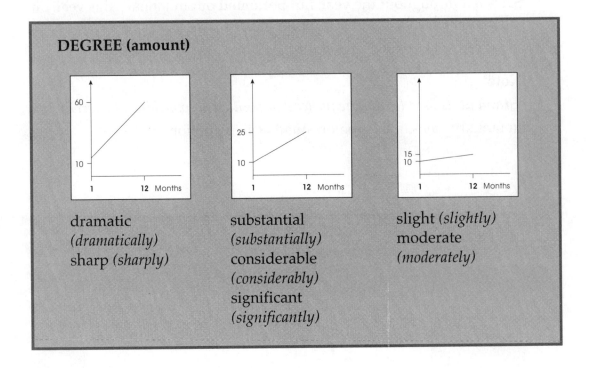

Speed

There has been a **rapid** increase in distribution costs in the last year.
The level of investment rose **suddenly** last year.
There has been a **steady** decline in share prices on the London Stock Exchange.

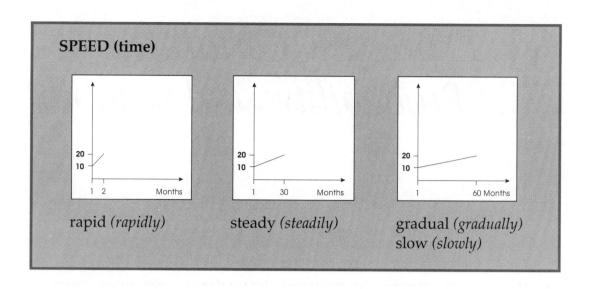

Market activity

The stock market has been **buoyant** in the last couple of days.

Other examples

The property market is **stagnant** at the moment, nothing is moving. We hope it becomes more **active** soon.
Demand has been **sluggish** recently.
Prices have remained **steady** over the last year.

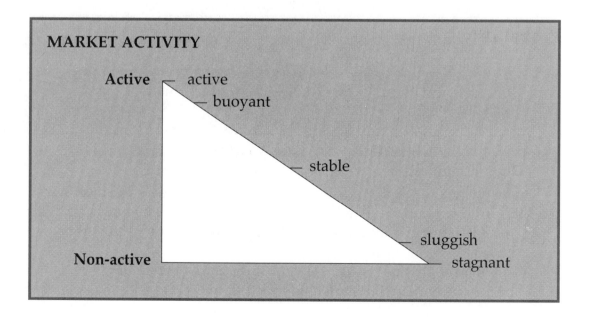

61 Expressing Certainty, Probability, and Possibility

Certainty

> The use of the new equipment **will certainly** increase costs.

Other examples

The programme **will definitely** be implemented next month.
The establishment of the new department is **certain to** make a big difference to the company.
This service **would** increase the amount of information available to clients.
We **shall definitely not** make any changes to the existing contract at the moment.
It is a very complex process. The staff are **bound to** need special training.

Probability

> The decision about the design project **should** be made at today's meeting.

Other examples

Jane phoned to say that she'll **probably** be a little late for the meeting.
It is **unlikely** that we shall be in a position to take on any new staff this year.
There's a letter in the post for you. It **ought to** arrive today. It was posted on Friday.
We will **probably not** issue a new brochure until next January.
The next meeting of the shareholders is **likely to** take place in September.

Possibility

> It is **possible** that the company may open a new branch in Moscow in the near future.

Other examples

Bob isn't sure whether he can attend the conference. He **may** be in Japan at that time.

We'll **possibly** appoint an extra accounts clerk in a month or two.

I don't know why Alan isn't here yet. He **could** have missed his connecting flight.

We **might** postpone the launch until later in the season but we haven't made a definite decision yet.

Restructure the department? While we're working on the current project, that is **impossible.**

CERTAINTY, PROBABILITY AND POSSIBILITY

	Verbs	Adverbs	Adjectives
Yes 100%	will / would	certainly / definitely	certain (to) / definite / bound to
↑	should / ought to	almost certainly / definitely	almost certain
	–	probably	probable / likely
	may / can	possibly	possible
	could / might	–	–
↓	–	probably not	improbable / unlikely
No 100%	will not / would not	certainly not / definitely not	certain not to / impossible

EVERYDAY COMMUNICATION

62 Forecasting

➡ We've experienced a lot of problems in the last few years, but now that Europe is finally coming out of recession, **I'm confident that** we'll achieve much greater success this year.

➡ We need to step up production. **I expect** the demand for these products to be much greater than in previous years.

➡ **I doubt if** we'll be able to make all the necessary changes to our information systems without employing extra staff.

➡ **I would be surprised if** we did not achieve sales of more than one million pounds.

➡ **We anticipate** profits of around fifty million dollars in the first six months of the year.

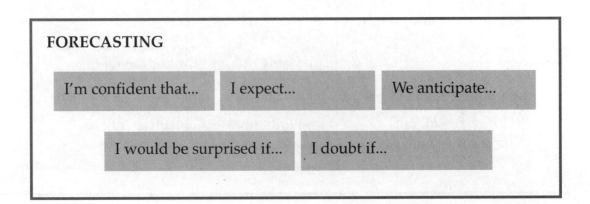

FORECASTING

I'm confident that...   I expect...   We anticipate...

I would be surprised if...   I doubt if...

63 Generalising

 As a rule, we expect payment in advance, but we are willing to make an exception in your case.

 Normally, fringe benefits are liable to tax, but there may be special circumstances when this is not so.

 I think we're all in agreement with Andy's suggestions **in principle**. However, we'll need to consider them in more detail before we make any definite decisions.

 We're here today to discuss our sales strategies **in general**, and sales in France in particular.

 We have had a very good year **on the whole**, despite the negative trends in January and February.

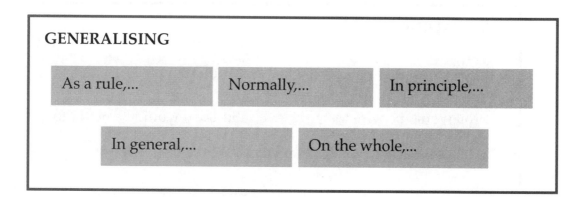

EVERYDAY COMMUNICATION

64 Persuading and Recommending

Persuading

 You've had so many break-ins recently, **can't I persuade you to** install a better security system?

 Wouldn't you agree that it's important to remember how the new production process will affect the environment?

 You'd be wise to consider getting a second opinion on this.

 Surely it would be better to redeploy some of our existing staff, rather than appoint extra people.

Note
To *'persuade'* is to reason with other people in order to make them do something you want them to do, often when they are reluctant to do it.

PERSUADING	
Can't I persuade you to...?	Wouldn't you agree that...?
You would be wise to consider...	Surely it would be better to...

256 EVERYDAY COMMUNICATION

Recommending

 I recommend that you review all the accounting systems at the end of this year.

 I think you should employ an outside consultant.

 We suggest that you change the procedures.

 It would be in your interest to wait for the Chairman's decision on this matter.

 We strongly recommend that you locate the new factory in an enterprise zone.

 You might like to consider investing in some new computer hardware.

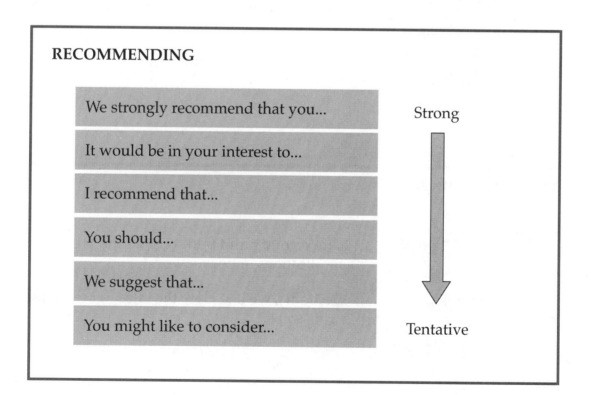

EVERYDAY COMMUNICATION

65 Sequencing

The first stage

First of all,

Firstly,

To start with,

We'll start

First of all, I'd like to demonstrate our new product to you.

Firstly, we should consider the proposals you have submitted.

To start with, I'd like to hear what you all think about the draft contract that I sent you last week.

We'll start in the Accounts Office, and then I'll introduce you to our secretarial staff.

The second stage

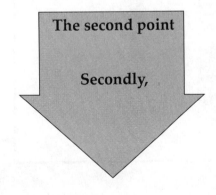

The second point

Secondly,

The second point is to consider the tax implications of this move.

Secondly, we'll analyse the sales figures of the last six months.

EVERYDAY COMMUNICATION

The next stage

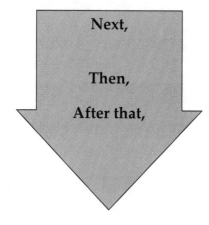

Next, I'd like to look at next year's production budget.

Then, I'll deal with our plans for next year.

After that, perhaps we could listen to David's ideas about our stand at the forthcoming Trade Fair.

The final stage

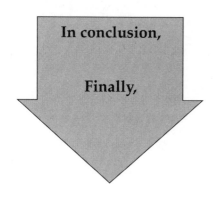

In conclusion, I'd like to return to a point I made earlier.

Finally, we'll look at the new materials that Sue has brought along to show us.

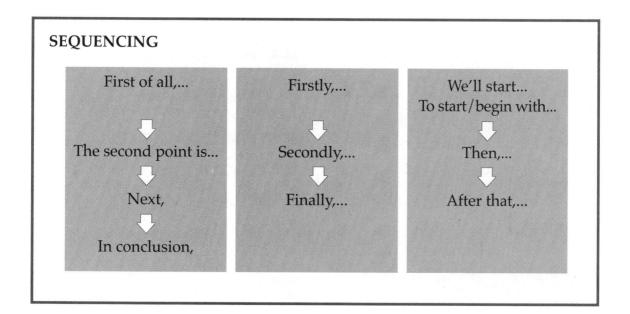

EVERYDAY COMMUNICATION

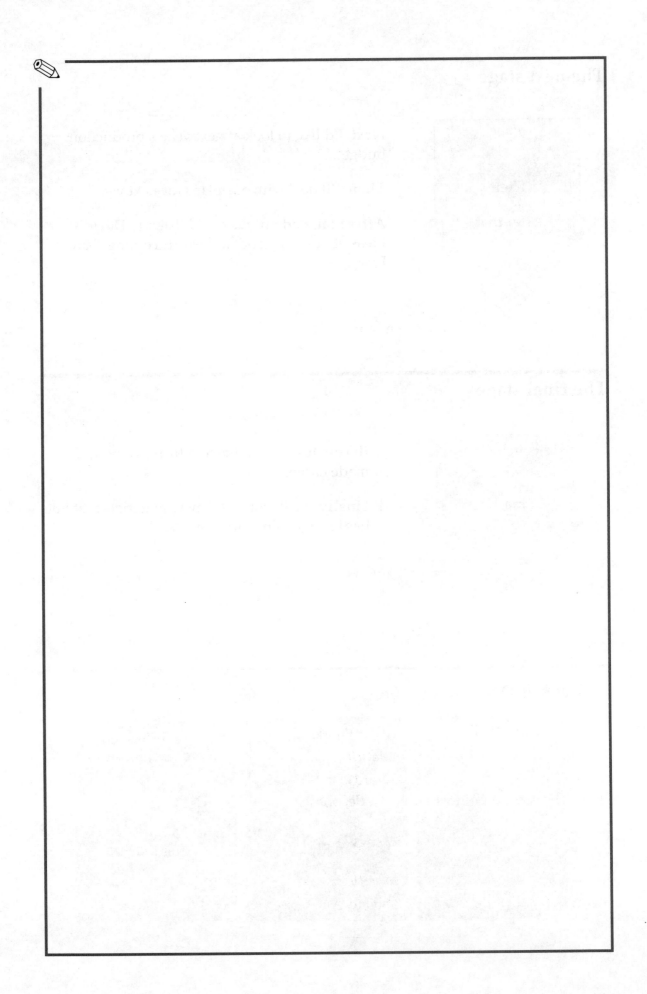

66 Help!
(What to Say if You Have Problems)

Asking someone to repeat something
Sorry?
Could you repeat that, please?
I'm sorry. I didn't quite catch that.

Saying you don't understand
I'm sorry. I didn't understand that.
I'm not sure if I've understood you correctly.

Asking someone to speak slowly
Could you speak a little more slowly, please?

Asking what a word means
What does _____ mean?

Saying you would like to ask a question
May I ask a question?

Asking someone to translate a word
How do you say _____ in English?

Asking how to spell something
How do you spell _____?

Asking how to pronounce something
How do you pronounce this word?

Saying you do not speak much English
I'm sorry, I only speak a little English.

Asking someone to explain something
Would you mind explaining this to me, please?

EVERYDAY COMMUNICATION

Business Skills

67 Telephoning

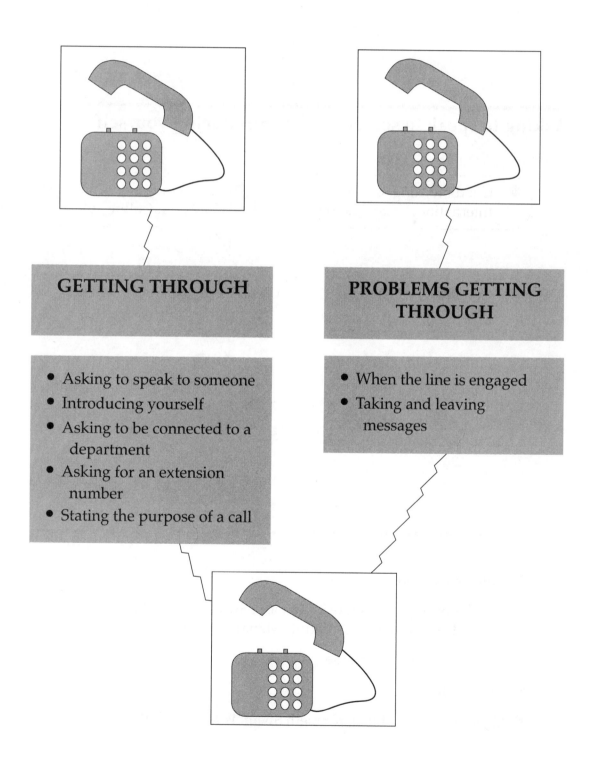

GETTING THROUGH

- Asking to speak to someone
- Introducing yourself
- Asking to be connected to a department
- Asking for an extension number
- Stating the purpose of a call

PROBLEMS GETTING THROUGH

- When the line is engaged
- Taking and leaving messages

68 Telephoning: Getting Through

Asking to speak to someone and introducing yourself

- ● Good morning. Carlton International. Can I help you?

- ▼ Good morning. **Can I speak to** Adam Collins, **please?**

- ● Certainly. Just a moment, please.

- ▼ Hello, Adam Collins.

> Can I speak to..., please?

- ● Philipsons. Good morning.
- ▼ Good morning. **My name is** Kenneth Swan of Swan Pharmaceuticals. **Could I speak to** your Accounts Manager, **please?**
- ● Yes. Just a moment, please.
- ■ Mr. Smith's office.
- ▼ Good morning. **This is** Kenneth Swan. Is Mr. Smith there?

266 BUSINESS SKILLS

- ■ Yes, one moment, **I'll put you through.**
- ◆ Hello Kenneth, how are you?

My name is...	Could I speak to..., please?
This is...	Is...there?
I'll put you through I'm putting you through	

- ▼ Madden Limited. May I help you?
- ● **I'd like to speak to** Bernard Robinson, **please**.
- ▼ Who's calling?
- ● **My name is** Hans Meyer. **I'm calling from** Hoechst AG in Frankfurt.
- ▼ Hold the line, please.
- ■ Bernard Robinson.
- ● Good morning, Mr. Robinson. **This is** Hans Meyer **of** Hoechst AG. I'm calling about our meeting next week.

I'd like to speak to..., please	My name is..., I'm calling from...
This is...of/from (Hoechst)	

❗ Typical Error	Correct
~~Here is Otto Schmidt.~~	**This is** Otto Schmidt. **My name is** Otto Schmidt.

TELEPHONING

In English-speaking countries, it is usual to give your full name with the forename before the surname:

My name is John Smith.
My name is Louise Walker.

When asking to speak to someone, it is usual to ask for them by their full name:

Can I speak to Robert Palmer, please?
Is Maria Fernandez there, please?

*You can also ask for a person by their title: **'Dr.'**, **'Mr.'**, **'Mrs.'** or **'Miss'**. (Other titles are not commonly used in English.)*

Can I speak to Mr. Richards, please?
Is Mrs. Field there, please?

Asking to be connected to a department

- Good afternoon. Simpsons.

▼ Good morning. **Could you put me through to** the Customer Services Department, **please?**

- Just a moment, please.

Could you put me through to... please?

- Masons. Good morning.
- Good morning. **Could I speak to someone in** the Accounts Department, **please?**
- Putting you through...
- Hello. Accounts.

Could I speak to someone in... please?

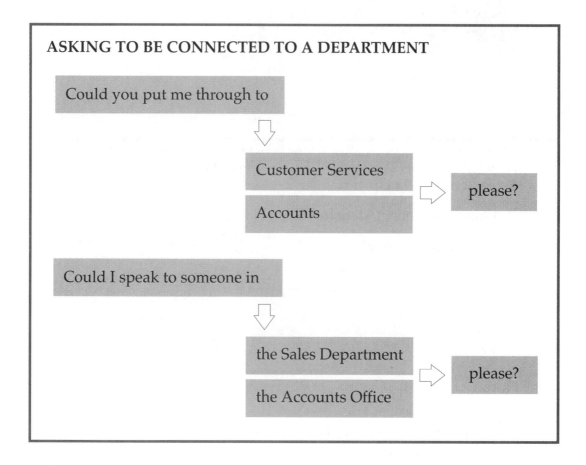

ASKING TO BE CONNECTED TO A DEPARTMENT

Could you put me through to → Customer Services / Accounts → please?

Could I speak to someone in → the Sales Department / the Accounts Office → please?

The telephone operator might want more information to decide which section of a large department should deal with your call. The operator might ask:
Could you tell me the purpose of your call, please?

TELEPHONING

Asking for an extension number

- Good morning. Anderson and Company. Can I help you?
- ▼ Good morning. **May I have extension number** 2142, **please?**
- Yes, certainly. Hold on, please.

> May I have extension number... please?

- Frasers. Can I help you?
- ▼ Good afternoon. **Extension** 306, **please**.
- Putting you through.

> Extension...please.

Note

Extension numbers
When the extension number is small, we say:
Extension **twenty-five**, please.

When the extension number is a round figure, we say:
Extension **four hundred**, please.

When the extension number is larger (three digits or more), we usually say each digit separately:
Extension **six-five-three** (653), please.

! Typical Error	Correct
~~Extension three hundred and sixteen, please.~~	**Extension 3-1-6, please.**

*On the telephone, we say **'o'** as in the letter **'o'**, **not** zero.*

*Sometimes, in the US **'zero'** is said.*

Stating the purpose of your call

- John Smith.
- ▼ Hello, Mr. Smith. This is Angela Coombes of Star Publishing.
- Hello, Mrs. Coombes. What can I do for you?
- ▼ **I'm calling about** the brochure. The design has been approved by our Marketing Director. Can we have a meeting next week to discuss the arrangements for printing and mailing?
- Yes, that's a good idea. How about Wednesday?
- ▼ That's fine for me. Are you free in the morning?
- Yes. Is ten o'clock all right for you?
- ▼ Yes, that's fine. I look forward to seeing you then.

> I'm calling about...

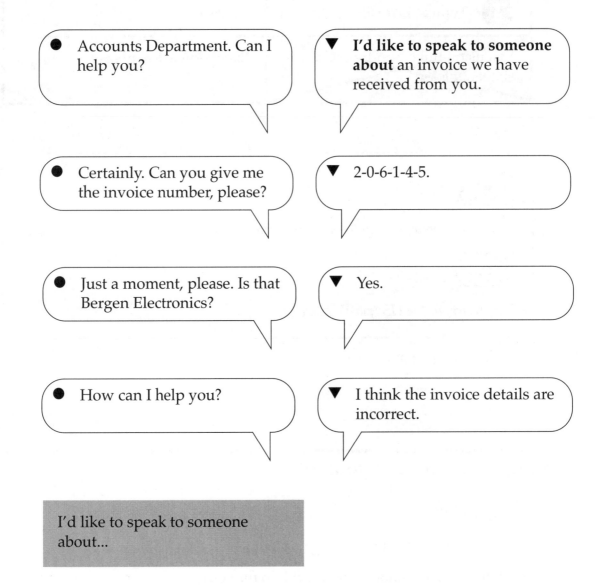

- Accounts Department. Can I help you?
- I'd like to speak to someone **about** an invoice we have received from you.
- Certainly. Can you give me the invoice number, please?
- 2-0-6-1-4-5.
- Just a moment, please. Is that Bergen Electronics?
- Yes.
- How can I help you?
- I think the invoice details are incorrect.

I'd like to speak to someone about...

- Good morning. Browns.
- Good morning, this is Roger Scott. Can I speak to Julia Smith, please?
- Julia Smith speaking.
- Hello Julia, **I wanted to know** what you thought about the new brochure?

I wanted to know...

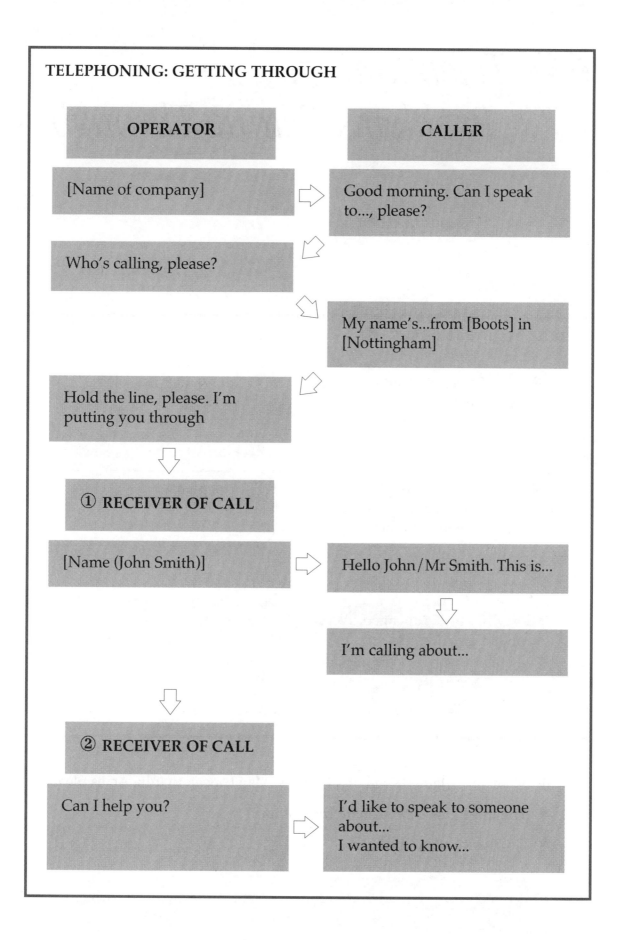

69 Telephoning: Problems Getting Through

When the line is engaged

- Sun Systems. Good morning. Can I help you?

▼ Margaret Jones, please.

- Putting you through.... **Sorry, her line is engaged. Would you like to hold on?**

▼ **Yes, please.**

| Sorry, her line is engaged. Would you like to hold on? | Yes, please |

- My name is James Keen of Simpsons. May I speak to Julia Acres, please?
- ▼ **The line's busy. Would you like to hold?**
- **No, thank you. I'll call back later.**

| The line's busy. Would you like to hold? | No, thank you. I'll call back later |

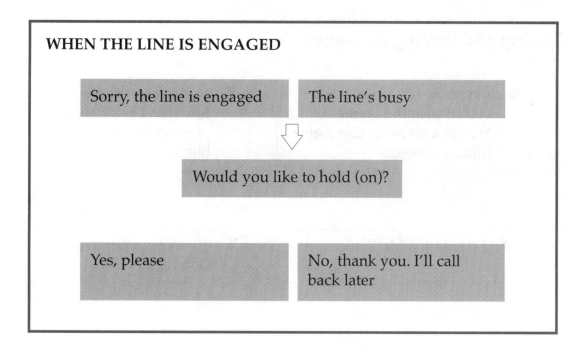

When the person you are calling is not in

- Good afternoon. This is Mary Adams. Could I speak to Mike French, please?
- ▼ **I'm sorry, he's not in the office at the moment.**
- **Do you know what time he'll be back?**
- ▼ **He should be back by** three-thirty.
- **I'll call again later**, then. Thank you.

| I'm sorry he/she is not in the office at the moment | Do you know what time he/she will be back? |
| He/she should be back by... | I'll call again... |

TELEPHONING

Taking and leaving messages

- **I'm sorry,** Mr. James **is not available at the moment.** He's in a meeting. **Can I give him a message?**

▼ Yes, please. **Would you tell him** that Geoff Banks phoned. I'd like to speak to him as soon as possible.

- I'll tell him, Mr. Banks.

▼ Thank you very much. Goodbye.

| I'm sorry...is not available at the moment. Can I give him a message? | Would you tell him...? |

- This is Anne Mason. Could I speak to Jill Smith, please?
- ▼ I'm sorry. She's not in the office at the moment.
- **Could you give her a message, please?**
- ▼ **Yes, certainly.**
- **Could you ask her to call me back, please?** She's got my number and I'll be in all day today and tomorrow.
- ▼ **Could you give me your name again, please?**
- **Yes, it's** Anne Mason. **That's** M-A-S-O-N.
- ▼ **I'll ask her to call you.**
- Thank you very much. Goodbye.

- Sales. May I help you?
- Yes. Good morning, this is Hilary Johnson. Could I speak to Martin Smith?
- I'm sorry he's with a customer at the moment. Can I give him a message?
- **I'm just returning his call.**
- Oh. Right. I'll tell him as soon as he's free.
- Thank you.

WHEN THE PERSON YOU ARE CALLING IS NOT IN

I'm sorry he/she is not in the office at the moment	Do you know what time he/she will be back?
He/she should be back by...	I'll call again...

TAKING MESSAGES

I'll ask him/her to call you back	Could you give me your name, please?
I'm sorry...is not available at the moment	Can I give him/her a message?

LEAVING MESSAGES

Could you give him/her a message?	Could you ask him/her to call me back?
Would you tell him/her...?	I'm returning his/her call

70 Presentations: Structure

Usual pattern of a presentation

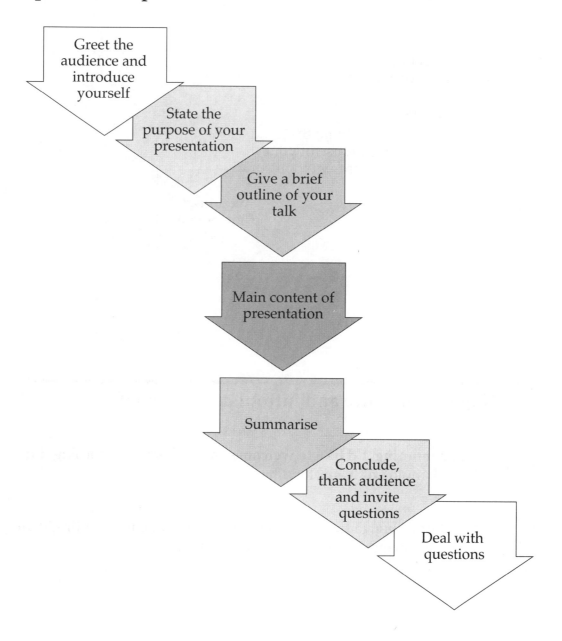

PRESENTATIONS

71 Presentations: Getting Started

Starting the presentation

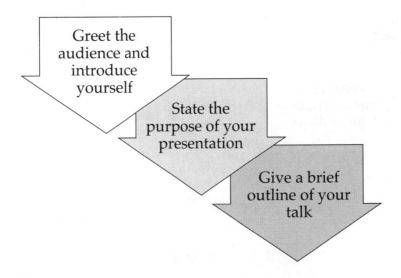

Greeting the audience and introducing yourself

➡ **Good morning. I'd like to welcome you** all here this morning. **I'm** Jane Hampton **of** Hampton Pharmaceuticals.

➡ **Good morning, ladies and gentlemen. My name is** Peter Bright **and I am the** Finance Director **of** Bright and Farnham.

Good afternoon, everyone. Thank you all for coming. Let me introduce myself. My name's Richard Harrison **and I am from** James Morgan and Company.

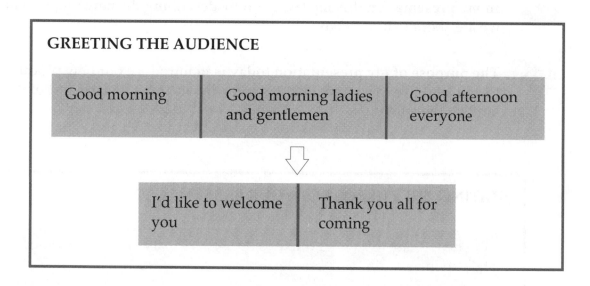

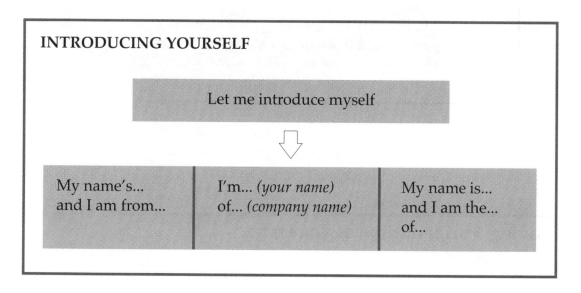

Stating the purpose of your presentation

 I'm here today to talk about the company's annual results.

 I'd like to speak briefly about our marketing campaign in Europe.

What I'd like to do today is to explain the production process to you.

 In my presentation this morning, I'll be describ**ing** the new project that we are about to undertake.

 The purpose of my presentation today is to introduce our new product to you, and to explain what it does and why we think it is the best of its kind on the market.

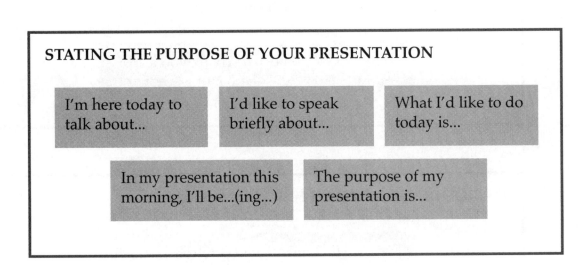

Giving a brief outline of your talk

I have divided my talk into three **main parts. Firstly,** I'd like to review the current situation in Europe. **Secondly,** I'll look at the markets in the US and Japan and, **finally,** I will talk about our plans for the future.

 I'll begin with some general comments about the company, **and then I'll deal with** each department in turn. **Then I'll move on to** financial matters. **After that,** we'll look at future trends.

 I'll be talking about three **main areas. First of all,** I'll describe the history of the company. **Then** I'll go on to talk about current business and **finally** I'll tell you about the future projects we are planning.

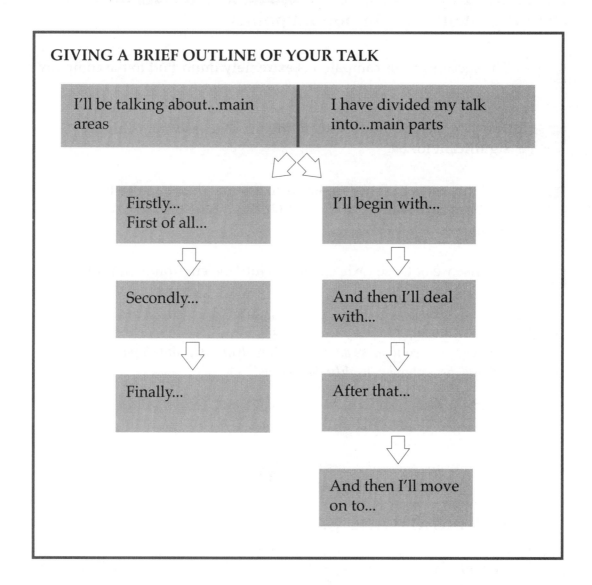

PRESENTATIONS

72 Presentations: The Main Part

Drawing attention to important points

 The success of this campaign is **extremely important** to the company.

 The increase in consumer spending over the last year is **highly significant** for us.

 So, I think it is **highly dangerous** to assume that, because this product has been successful up to now, it will continue to be so. We cannot be complacent.

 The release of these toxic chemicals into the environment is **totally unacceptable** to us.

Note
*Adverbs can be used to make adjectives more **dramatic** and emphasise their importance, for example: '**highly** dangerous'.*

See also *Adverbs and Adjectives* (Unit 28).

DRAWING ATTENTION TO IMPORTANT POINTS

| extremely important | highly significant | highly dangerous | totally unacceptable |

Referring to visuals

I'd like you to have a look at this bar chart, which shows our UK profits for the last five years.

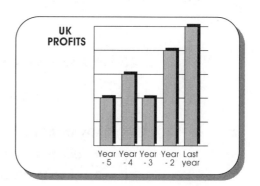

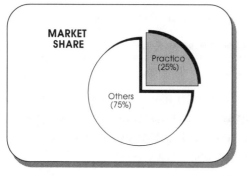

As you can see from this pie chart, we have a twenty-five per cent share of the total market at the moment.

If you could look at this graph, you will see that sales increased significantly last year.

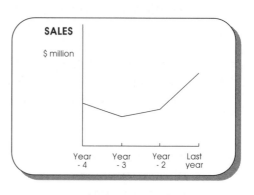

	10 years ago	5 years ago	Now
Management	12	44	150
Sales persons	18	62	217
Skilled workers	90	177	466
Unskilled	320	341	293
Part-time	2	24	98
	442	648	1,224

The figures in this table show how the number of employees in this company has grown over the past ten years. As you will see, staff numbers have almost tripled in ten years.

REFERRING TO VISUALS

| I'd like you to have a look at... | As you can see from... | If you could look at... | The figures in this table show... |

PRESENTATIONS

Highlighting advantages and disadvantages

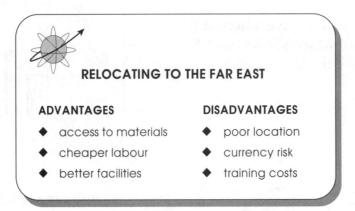

➡ **The benefit of** relocating to the Far East is that we would have better access to raw materials. **Other advantages are** that labour is cheaper and in general, the facilities are better. **The disadvantages are** the poor location, the currency risk and the high training costs.

➡ I've outlined three possible courses of action. Now, **what are the advantages** of each one? Well, **I tend to favour** the first option, hiring temporary staff, **because** expenditure will be lower.

➡ There are two alternatives as I have explained. Obviously, the second option - to invest in government bonds, is attractive, but **there are some disadvantages.**

HIGHLIGHTING ADVANTAGES AND DISADVANTAGES

ADVANTAGES	DISADVANTAGES
What are the advantages?	There are some disadvantages
I tend to favour...because...	The disadvantages are...
The benefit of...is...	
Other advantages are...	

BUSINESS SKILLS

Changing to another topic

 So, we've looked at the various problems and **I'd now like to consider** some possible solutions.

 Having looked at all the possible options, **let's move on to** the advantages and disadvantages of each one.

 This leads me to my next point which is the question of attracting more investment.

CHANGING TO ANOTHER TOPIC

| I'd now like to consider... | Let's move on to... | This leads me to my next point... |

Using rhetorical questions

 Over the last two years, there has been a considerable drop in profits. **What was the reason for this**? Obviously, the economic recession throughout Europe was a key factor.

 It has been decided to make some structural changes in the company. **How will this affect** our department? Well, unfortunately it will result in some redundancies.

 If you look at this chart, you will see that this study has taken far longer than we would have liked. **How can we explain this?**

 So, as I mentioned earlier, there is a great demand for this type of product in Japan. **What, then are the implications for** our company? Well, we intend to appoint local agents in Tokyo.

Note

*A **rhetorical question** is a question to which we do not expect to get an answer. The speaker will answer the question him/herself. It is just used for effect. It is useful in a presentation because it involves the audience and helps to link points in the presentation.*

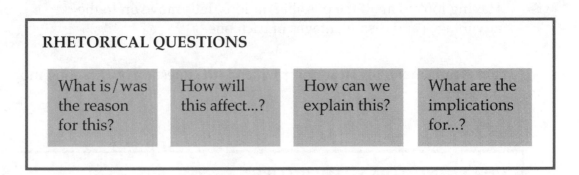

Referring to other parts of the presentation

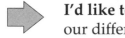 **I'd like to go back to a point I mentioned earlier,** the performance of our different brands.

 As I've already said, increasing our market share is one of our top priorities in the coming year.

 Since five years ago, the number of people employed in this department has risen by ten per cent. **I'll come back to this point in a moment** but I'd like to look now at the total increase in employees in the company as a whole.

 If you wouldn't mind, **I'll deal with** questions **later**.

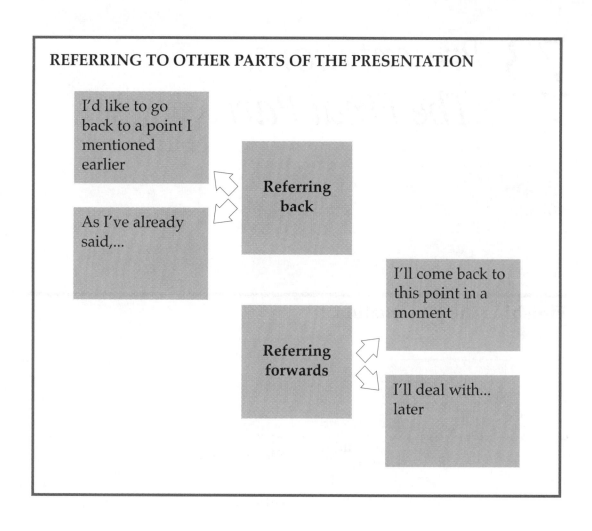

73 Presentations: The Final Part

Finishing the presentation

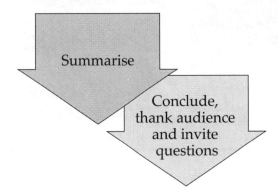

Summarising

 To summarise the main points of my talk, we have to become more competitive. We must also consider the development of new products. Finally, we have to be more profitable.

To sum up, then, we must reduce our personnel costs, and to do this, we must cut the size of the workforce.

 At this stage, I'd like to run through my main points again.

SUMMARISING

| To sum up... | To summarise the main points of my talk... | At this stage, I'd like to run through... |

Concluding

 I'd like to conclude by reminding you of something I said at the beginning of my talk.

 That brings me to the end of my presentation, ladies and gentlemen. I hope you found it interesting. **I'd like to thank you for your attention.**

 I've summarised my talk in these handouts which I'll distribute now. **Thank you for listening.**

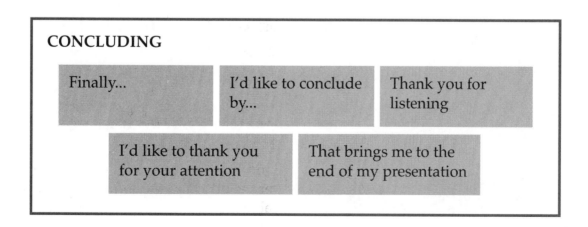

Inviting questions

 I'd like to thank you for your attention. **Now, if there are any questions, I'll be pleased to answer them.**

 Thank you for listening. **If you have any questions, I'd be happy to answer them.**

 Thank you all for your attention. **If there are any questions, I'll do my best to answer them.**

INVITING QUESTIONS

Now, if there are any questions, I'll be pleased to answer them	If you have any questions, I'd be happy to answer them	If there are any questions, I'll do my best to answer them

PRESENTATIONS

74 Presentations: Dealing with Questions

Clarifying questions before answering

- What made you decide to centre your operations on Milan and Amsterdam? Don't you think Paris would have been a better choice?
- ▼ **If I understand the question correctly, you would like to know** the criteria we used to choose the bases for our European operations.

- I'd like to know about the cuts you mentioned.
- ▼ **I'm sorry. I didn't hear you. Would you mind repeating your question?**

- Are you planning to expand your business in South America?
- ▼ **Do you mean** in South America generally, or in Brazil, where we are at present?

CLARIFYING QUESTIONS

| If I understand the question correctly, you would like to know... | I'm sorry. I didn't hear you. Would you mind repeating your question? | Do you mean...? |

Avoiding giving an answer

- How can you be sure that the development of this product will not be detrimental to the environment?
  ▼ **I'm afraid I'm not the right person to give you an answer to that question.**

- Is it true that you are closing down your Paris branch in the near future?
  ▼ **I'm afraid I'm not able to answer that question at present.**

AVOIDING GIVING AN ANSWER

| I'm afraid I'm not the right person to give you an answer to that question | I'm afraid I'm not able to answer that question at present |

Showing tactful disagreement

- I can't understand why this project has been given higher priority than the market research project. That is far more important in my opinion.
  ▼ **Yes, I see your point, but** I know you will appreciate how important it is to keep up to date with product development.

- Wouldn't it be a good idea to recruit locally for this project?
  ▼ **Well I have some doubts about that.** It would be difficult to recruit local people with the right experience.

SHOWING TACTFUL DISAGREEMENT

| Yes, I see your point, but... | Well I have some doubts about that |

It would be unusual for a presenter to show strong disagreement with a question. Disagreement in British English often starts with a tactful phrase, for example: "I see your point, but...".

Giving reassurance

- I think we are all very concerned about waste products from the factory and how they will affect the local atmosphere.

▼ **You need have no worries on that point. I can assure you that** proper safety precautions are in hand.

- Can you guarantee that the transfer of the bottling plant to your factory in the north will not cause a major unemployment problem in this area?

▼ **I can understand your concern, but** we will be creating new jobs in other departments and this will mean that there will be very few redundancies.

GIVING REASSURANCE

| You need have no worries on that point | I can assure you that... | I can understand your concern, but... |

BUSINESS SKILLS

PRESENTATIONS

75 Meetings: Structure

The structure of meetings

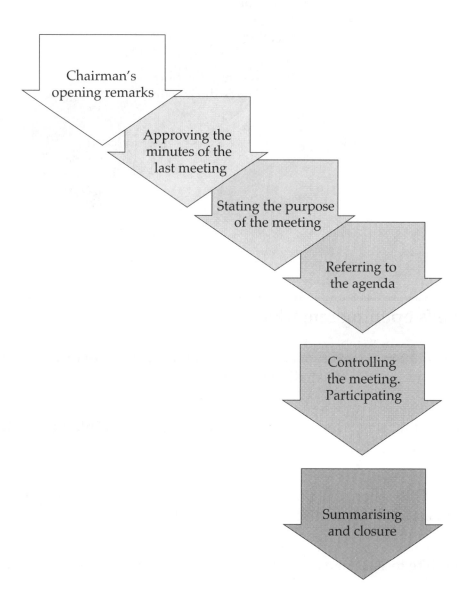

76 Chairing a Meeting

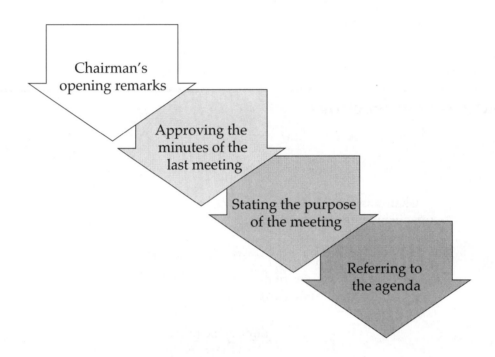

Chairman's opening remarks

 Good morning, everyone. **Thank you all for getting here so promptly.** Now we're all here, **shall we begin?**

 Good morning, everyone. **We're all here now so I think we should get started.**

 Good afternoon. I'm glad you could all make it today. We've got a lot of important things to discuss. So, **let's get down to business.**

 I'd like to welcome Diana Crawley, who is a newcomer to the meeting.

I have received apologies for absence from Tim Best and Richard Langham, who are away on business in Sweden this week.

Note
*The person who takes charge of a meeting is called **'the chairperson'** or the **'chair'**, and sometimes the **'chairman'**.*

OPENING REMARKS

Let's get started, shall we?	Shall we begin?
Let's get down to business	Thank you all for getting here so promptly
We're all here now so I think we should get started	I'd like to welcome…

I have received apologies for absence from…

Approving the minutes

 I think you've all received the minutes of our last meeting which was in September. **Can I take it (that) you've all read them? Are there any matters arising from the minutes?**

 Has everyone seen the minutes of the last meeting? **Can I sign the minutes?**

Note
When the chairperson signs the minutes of the previous meeting, everyone is agreeing formally that the minutes are an accurate record of what was discussed.

MEETINGS

APPROVING THE MINUTES

Can I take it (that) you've all read the minutes?

Are there any matters arising from the minutes?

Can I sign the minutes?

Stating the purpose of the meeting: (informal meetings)

 We're here today to decide on a strategy for the product launch in June.

 The aim of this meeting is to review sales in the last six months and to discuss our plans for the next six months.

 I called this meeting to bring you up to date with the latest developments in the research project.

Note

Formal meetings have pre-set agendas. At less formal meetings, the chairperson usually reminds participants of the purpose of the meeting.

STATING THE PURPOSE OF THE MEETING

We're here today to...

The aim of this meeting is...

I called this meeting to...

Referring to the agenda and inviting contributions

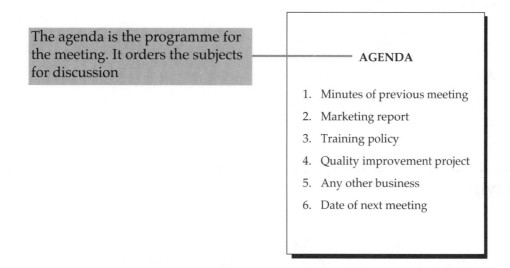

The agenda is the programme for the meeting. It orders the subjects for discussion

AGENDA

1. Minutes of previous meeting
2. Marketing report
3. Training policy
4. Quality improvement project
5. Any other business
6. Date of next meeting

 Let's begin with item number two, the marketing report.

 As you can see, the first item on the agenda is the appointment of an additional member of staff to the department. **Perhaps you'd like to** give us some more information on this, Anne.

 I hope you've all received the agenda. The first point we have to consider is the testing of the prototype. **Would you like to open the discussion,** Dr. Humphries?

REFERRING TO THE AGENDA AND INVITING CONTRIBUTIONS

| I hope you've all received the agenda | As you can see, the first item on the agenda is... | The first point we have to consider is... |
| Perhaps you'd like to... | Would you like to open the discussion,...? | Let's begin with... |

MEETINGS

77 Controlling the Meeting

Moving on

 Thank you, Mr. Taylor. **Could we now move on to item two on the agenda**, which is to set a date for the press conference?

 I think we have discussed this item for long enough. **Can we move on then to the next item on the agenda,** item 6?

 I don't want us to spend any more time on this item. So **unless anyone has something important to add, can we move on please** to the next item on the agenda?

 Can we take item 6 now, please? That is to look at targets for next year.

MOVING ON

Could we now move on to item... on the agenda?	Can we move on then to the next item on the agenda?
Unless anyone has something important to add, can we move on please?	Can we take item... now, please?

Inviting reactions

 So, John is suggesting making cuts in the marketing department. **What are your views on this,** Martin?

 I should like to hear the views of the sales department. Colin, **what do you have to say** about this proposed pricing structure?

 This is such an important issue that **I should like to go round the table and ask each of you in turn for your views.**

 Thank you for your report, Anthony. **Does anyone have anything they would like to say** about what Anthony has just said?

- Michael, **you look as though you would like to say something** about this.
- ▼ Thank you. Yes, I would like to make the point that...

INVITING REACTIONS

What are your views on this?	What do you have to say...?
I should like to go round the table and ask each of you in turn...	Does anyone have anything they would like to say?
	You look as though you would like to say something

MEETINGS

Keeping control of the meeting

We seem to be getting sidetracked here. **Could we get back to the main point, please?**

I'm sorry, Simon. This isn't really relevant to the discussion. **Could you stick to the subject, please?**

I would like this meeting to end by one o'clock at the latest, so **can we keep our comments brief and to the point, please?**

KEEPING CONTROL OF THE MEETING

Could we get back to the main point, please?

Could you stick to the subject, please?

Can we keep our comments brief and to the point, please?

Dealing with interruptions

- I think we should sell the land and...
- ▼ That's ridiculous! We can't do that, we...
- ■ **Just a moment,** David. **We'll come to you in a minute.**
- So, as I was saying. We should sell the land and buy another site for the factory.

Note

In formal meetings, participants normally only make comments through the chairperson. If someone reacts to a colleague without speaking through the chair, the chairperson may say:

Mr. Jones, **would you please address your remarks through the chair?**

DEALING WITH INTERRUPTIONS

Just a moment,... We'll come to you in a minute

Inviting votes and asking for consensus: (formal meetings)

 The proposal is that we should consider setting up an office in Leipzig. **Can we take a vote on this? Can I ask for a show of hands** in support of the proposal...and those against?

 So we have to decide whether to begin the project in June or whether to wait until the autumn. **Perhaps we should vote on this. Please raise your hand if you are in favour of** starting in June. ... Now, raise your hand if you are in favour of a delay until the autumn.

 So Jane has suggested that we begin the project next month. **Are we all agreed on that?**

INVITING VOTES AND ASKING FOR CONSENSUS

Can we take a vote on this?	Can I ask for a show of hands?
Perhaps we should vote on this	Please raise your hands if you are in favour of...

Are we all agreed on that?

Asking for clarification

 Sorry, Liz. **I'm not quite clear about what you've just said. Could you go over it again, please?**

 Could you please give us some more details of your plan?

 Could I just stop you for a moment? **I'm sorry but I didn't quite follow what you said about** the additives. **Would you mind going over it again?**

ASKING FOR CLARIFICATION

- I'm not quite clear about what you've just said
- I'm sorry but I didn't quite follow what you said about...
- Could you please give us some more details of...
- Could you go over it again, please?
- Would you mind going over it again?

Asking for any other business

● Right, I think we've covered all the items on the agenda. So, **does anyone have any other business they would like to raise?**

▼ Yes, I have one small point.

ASKING FOR ANY OTHER BUSINESS

Does anyone have any other business they would like to raise?

78 Participating in a Meeting

Structuring your argument

 I'd like to make three main points. **Firstly,** we should review the salary structure throughout the company. **Secondly,** we need to upgrade our management training programme. **Finally,** we should perhaps introduce an incentive scheme for the production workers. So, to concentrate on the salary structure first, I think...

 As I see it, **there are several advantages in** buying this particular machine. It is much more efficient than the existing one and it also has more functions. **The disadvantage is** that it would cost a great deal of money to install.

 The problem, as I see it, **is** manpower. **There are two possible solutions. One is** to appoint extra staff on temporary contracts. **Alternatively,** we could extend the hours of the existing staff and offer them a financial incentive.

 We need to decide on the location for the new plant. **One possibility is** to locate it next to the Head Office site as we have enough land there to do that. **On the other hand,** we could establish the plant near the existing warehouse. There are obvious advantages in choosing the second option.

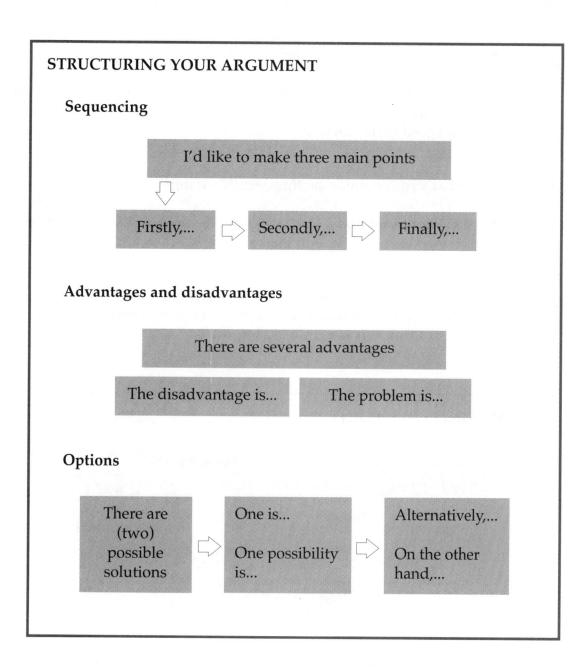

Making your point

- Would you like to comment on this, Mr. Yates?

▼ Personally, **I think it's important to remember** how much we have already invested in this project.

- What do you think, Adrian?
- Well, **as I see it**, our customers don't worry too much about the price. They are more concerned about the quality of the product and with our speed of delivery.

- What's your opinion on this, Mrs. Manning?
- **I'm convinced that** a joint venture is the answer. We already have very good connections in that area.

I'd like to make a point here. We are concentrating too much on our competitors. What we should be thinking about is the quality of our products. **I think this is extremely important.**

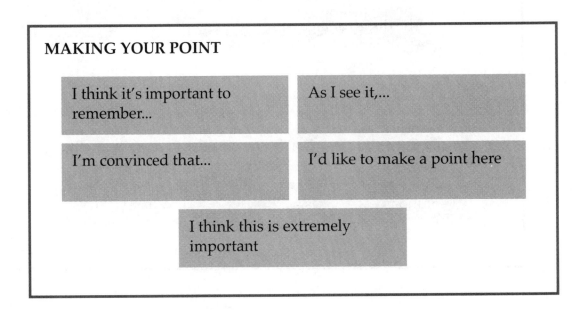

Reacting positively

- I propose that we transfer Jim Simmonds to Sales, and appoint two new recruits to start in January.
- **That seems like a good idea.**

- My feeling is that we ought to invest in a three month option which will yield a higher rate of interest. What do you think, Phil?

▼ **I've no objections to that.**

- So I think we should install the new machine in the factory next month.

▼ **Yes, and** we'll need to start training the operators immediately.

REACTING POSITIVELY

| That seems like a good idea | I've no objections to that | Yes, and... |

Reacting negatively

- I think we should change our approach to this problem. We should cut our losses and get out of that market altogether. It's always been more trouble than it's worth.

▼ Well, **I'm sorry, I don't agree.** This area has always been an important source of business to us, despite the problems involved.

- Perhaps we should change our advertising strategy and make more use of mail shots. What do you think?

▼ **I'm sorry. I really don't think that would work.** We wouldn't be targeting the kind of people we want to attract.

- There's no doubt that there is great export potential for our products in the States.

▼ **Yes, but** we mustn't concentrate solely on that area.

MEETINGS

In English, a negative reaction is often made more diplomatic by adding 'I'm afraid' or 'I'm sorry':
I'm afraid I don't agree.
I'm sorry. I can't go along with that idea.

REACTING NEGATIVELY

| I'm sorry, I don't agree | I'm sorry, I really don't think that would work | Yes, but... |

Interrupting

- So, I think we've considered all the possibilities now.

▼ **Can I say something?** I think we're forgetting the fact that our lease on the Basle office expires in two years' time. We might be able to cut our overheads by renting cheaper premises elsewhere.

- In order to maintain a competitive edge, I think we should reduce our prices in the autumn. It looks as if the customers will react favourably to lower prices and...

▼ **Excuse me, but** I really don't think it's advisable to reduce prices. Surely, the answer would be to target a different sector of the market.

- Well, I think we just have to acccept the fact that everyone in this industry is experiencing hard times at the moment. It's depressing but things will pick up later on,...

▼ **Sorry to interrupt, but** surely we should be thinking about increasing investments even though times are bad at present.

INTERRUPTING

| Can I say something? | Excuse me, but... | Sorry to interrupt, but... |

Clarification

- I suggest that we cut the advertising budget by £10,000.
- **Are you saying** that we should cut the combined advertising and sales promotion budget by £10,000?
- No, I'm suggesting that we keep the total budget the same but spend £10,000 less on advertising, and £10,000 more on sales promotion.

- I think our responsibilities should be divided up more clearly. At the moment, we've all got too many fingers in lots of different pies.
- **I'm sorry. I don't follow you.**
- **What I mean is,** we should each have a different area of responsibility, rather than each person being involved in lots of different areas without responsibility for any one of them.

- We're trying to attract the younger generation. I suggest that we use a geometric design in bright, primary colours for the boxes, maybe red and yellow. For the bottles, I'd like to have the same design but in different colours, perhaps blue and purple.
- **I'm sorry. I didn't quite catch that.**
- **I'll just run through it again.** Red and yellow for the boxes, blue and purple for the bottles but using the same design.

- **When you say** 'the Asia region', **do you mean** the whole of Asia, or just South-East Asia?
- Oh, I mean South-East Asia. **Let me explain,** this region is very important to us because...

MEETINGS

ASKING FOR CLARIFICATION

| Are you saying…? | I'm sorry. I don't follow you |
| I'm sorry. I didn't quite catch that | When you say…, do you mean…? |

CLARIFYING

| What I mean is… | I'll just run through it again |

Let me explain

MEETINGS

79 The End of the Meeting

Summarising

I'll just go over what we've agreed today. We've decided to start work on the new project immediately. John will make all the necessary arrangements with the Production Department. I'll contact James, and Susan will type up and distribute the specifications.

I think that covers everything. **So, to summarise,** there are two areas for action. We'll implement the new scheme immediately and David will draw up a draft contract for Nelsons.

SUMMARISING

| I'll just go over what we've agreed today | So, to summarise,... |

Closing the meeting

Has anyone got anything else to add?... All right then, **I think we can end the meeting now.** Thank you all for your contributions.

BUSINESS SKILLS

If no one has anything else to add, **I think we can bring the meeting to a close.**

 Thank you everyone, **that has been a most useful meeting. I hope to see you all again** in two months' time.

 The next meeting will be on 8th September. I look forward to seeing you all then.

 I declare the meeting closed. Thank you all for coming.

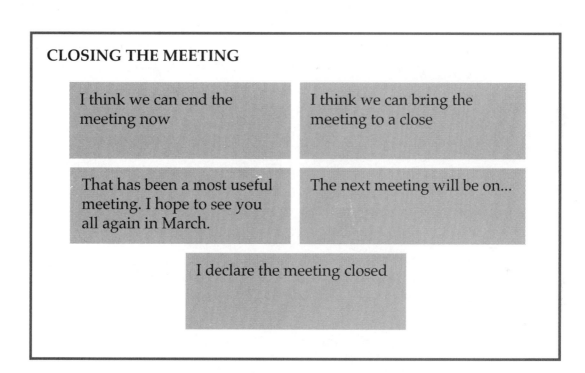

80 Negotiations: Structure

The usual structure of a negotiation

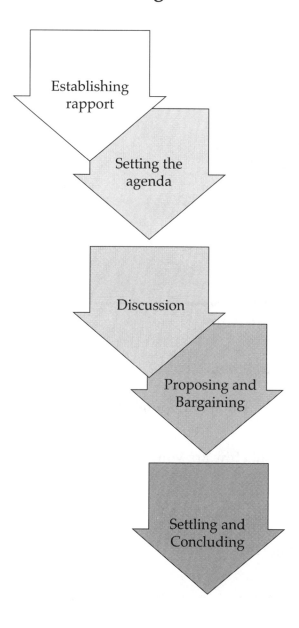

81 Negotiations: Getting Started

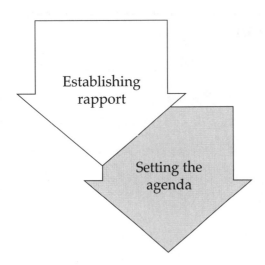

Establishing rapport: greetings

- ● Good morning, Mr. Brown.

- ▼ Good morning, Mr. Schiller. **It's good to see you again. How are you?**

- ● I'm fine, thank you. How are you?

- ● Hello John. It's been a long time. **Good to see you again.**

- ▼ **And you,** Martin. **How are you?**

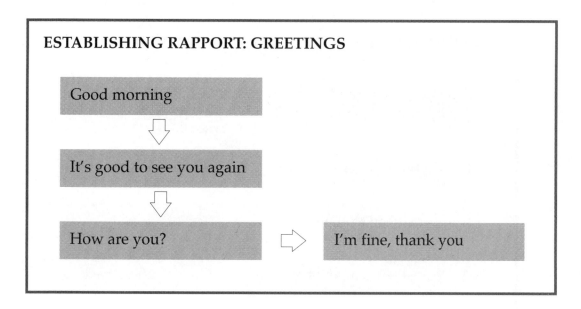

Talking about the journey and the visit

- **Did you have a good flight?**
- ▼ **Yes, thank you.** It was fine.
- **Is this your first visit to** England?
- ▼ **Yes, it is.** But I fly back to Vienna tonight.
- It's a pity you won't have time to do any sightseeing.

- **Have you been to** this part of Italy **before**?
- ▼ **Yes, I have**, but it's changed quite a lot since I was last here five years ago. I've noticed there are far more industrial buildings around here now.
- Yes, there are. **Are you staying here long?**
- ▼ **No, I'm going back** straight after our meeting.

TALKING ABOUT THE JOURNEY AND THE VISIT

Did you have a good flight/journey?	⇨	Yes, thank you
Is this your first visit to...?	⇨	Yes, it is/No, it isn't
Have you been to...before?	⇨	Yes, I have/No, I haven't
Are you staying here long?	⇨	No, I'm going back...

Asking about a colleague

- ● **How are things in** Germany?
- ▼ **Fine.** We're very busy at the moment.
- ● I met your colleague Joachim Kunz in Hamburg a few weeks ago.
- ▼ Oh yes. He works in our marketing department but in the same building as me.
- ● **Give him my regards** when you see him.
- ▼ Yes, I'll do that.

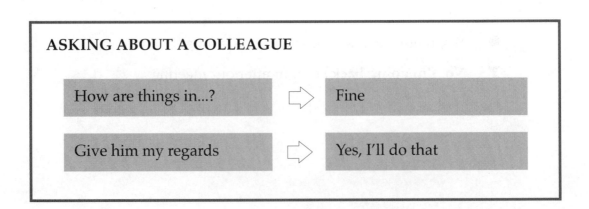

Small talk

*Before getting down to business, it is usual in most cultures to spend a short time making **'small talk'** with negotiating counterparts. It helps towards establishing a positive negotiating climate.*

If you have not met your counterparts before, you will also need to be introduced to them or to introduce yourself.

See also *Introductions* (Unit 54).

Setting the agenda

First of all, I think we should set the agenda for today's meeting. As you know, **the reason for being here is** to discuss your products and to see whether they will meet our requirements. **I would suggest that we start by** outlining our needs **and then perhaps** you could tell us how you think your products would meet those needs. **Do you agree with this?**

May we start by agreeing a procedure for our meeting today? **I suggest that, firstly**, each participant states his or her overall objectives. **After that**, perhaps we can clarify any areas of uncertainty. **Then, we'll go on to** discuss whether we can benefit from collaboration in certain areas as business partners. **Is that acceptable to you?**

I think we should begin by talking over the details of your offer to buy our company without discussing price. **We'll then move on to** negotiating the price, provided all the other details are agreed.

NEGOTIATIONS

In the UK/US, as in other countries, negotiations can be either in a formal meeting (with a chairperson) or in an informal meeting.

Setting the agenda
At the beginning of some negotiations, (especially ones with only a few participants), the participants agree on the procedure before starting to negotiate.

In more formal negotiations, as in official meetings, an agenda has probably been agreed in advance.

SETTING THE AGENDA

Suggesting the setting of the agenda

- First of all, I think we should set the agenda
- May we start by agreeing a procedure?
- The reason for being here is...

Sequencing

I would suggest that we start by...	...and then perhaps...
I suggest that, firstly,...	After that,...
I think we should begin by...	We'll then move on to... Then, we'll go on to...

BUSINESS SKILLS

Asking for agreement

Do you agree with this?

Is that acceptable to you?

Does that seem acceptable to you all?

82 Negotiations: The Discussion Phase

Stating and prioritising interests

➡ **The most important issue for us is** expansion in Europe. **We're particularly interested in** establishing subsidiaries in central Europe.

➡ **Our main priority is** to ensure that the new construction programme does not have a detrimental effect on the environment. **We think** this aspect **is vitally important**.

➡ **Our main interest is** to find new distributors in the Middle East. **We are also keen to** develop the existing distribution network in Europe, but **this is of a lower priority** at the moment.

➡ **We would** eventually **like to** introduce a franchise operation in the Far East, but **it is even more important to** develop the existing business in Europe.

Note
In large, formal negotiations, each participant normally states the interests and priorities of the country/company she/he is representing.

BUSINESS SKILLS

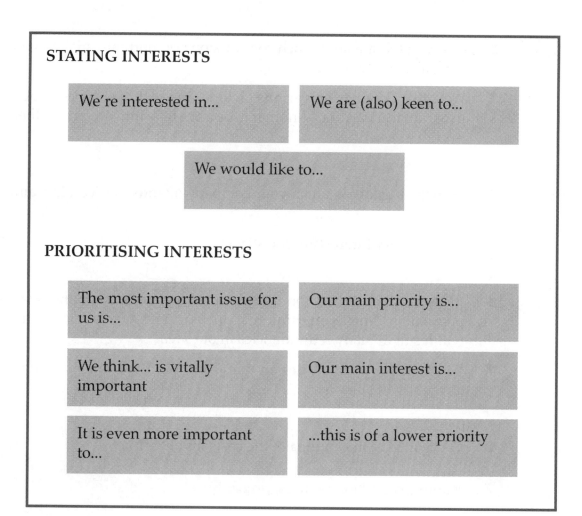

Questions and answers

- **I wonder if you could tell us** a little more about your plans for expanding into central Europe. Are you planning to set up subsidiaries, or agencies?
- ▼ **I'm afraid I can't give you an answer to that question at the moment.** We haven't made a choice yet between these two options.

- **How important is** the package design **to you?**
- ▼ Well, we are targeting the teenage market, so **it's vital** that we get the design right. They won't buy anything that isn't up to the minute, so the packaging has to look modern.

- **Can you tell me** how much commission you normally give to your agents?
  - ▼ Well, **that depends on various factors.** One of these factors is the geographical position. Another aspect we take into account is their overall sales in a year.

- **I'd like to ask** how much your company intends to invest in training this year.
  - ▼ **That's a very interesting question.**

- We're very concerned about the effect of this decision on the local population. **Don't you think that** opening a new factory in the north will result in many redundancies in our area?
  - ▼ **You need have no worries on that front.** We don't anticipate that any jobs will be lost.

- **Can you give me an idea** of the costs involved?
  - ▼ **About** two million pounds, probably.

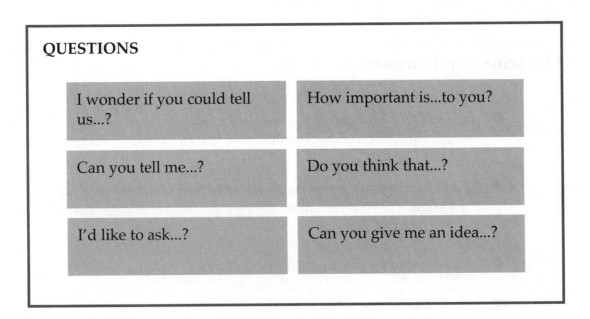

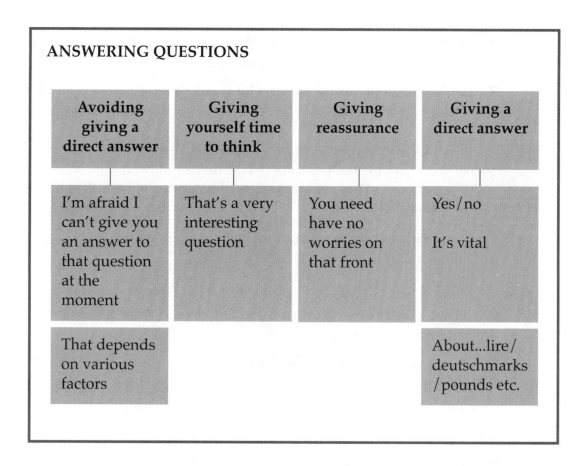

Clarifying and checking information

- **Am I right in thinking that** you're interested in purchasing the new machinery from a French company?
- ▼ **That's right, yes.** We are planning to get it from a company based in Rouen.

- **I'm not sure that I understood you correctly.** Are you interested in increasing the range of products that you are offering to the Chinese market?
- ▼ **Yes, that's correct.**

- **Would it be correct to say that** the American market is of less importance to you than the Middle East?
▼ At the moment, **yes.**

- **Could I just recap** on your main points? You are offering a discount of twenty per cent on orders of five thousand or more, and a discount of ten per cent on orders of between two and five thousand. **Is that right?**
▼ **No, that's not quite right.** It's fifteen per cent on orders of five thousand or more, not twenty per cent.

- **What exactly do you mean by** saying that our machine is too sophisticated for your needs?
▼ **Let me make it a bit clearer.** We need something which is simpler to operate because our staff are not very highly skilled, they couldn't handle anything too complex.

- **When you say** 'demand is falling', **do you mean** throughout the world, or in specific markets?
▼ **What I meant to say was that** demand in Europe is falling.

CLARIFYING AND CHECKING INFORMATION

Am I right in thinking that...?	I'm not sure that I understood you correctly...
Would it be correct to say that...?	Could I just recap...?
What exactly do you mean by...?	When you say..., do you mean..?

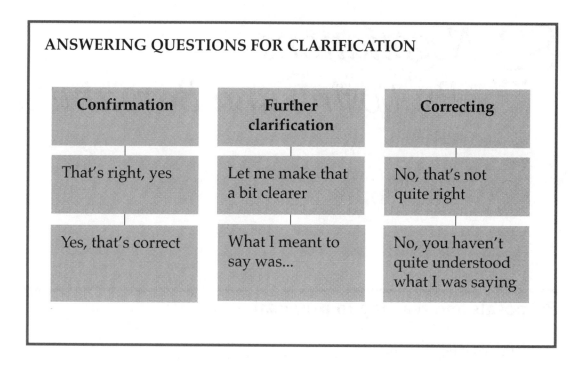

83 Negotiations: Proposing and Bargaining

Proposals and reacting to proposals

(Internal negotiation)

- At the moment, our Head Office in London deals with all the administrative procedures. As we now have both a factory and a warehouse in the north of England, **we propose that** a regional office be established in Manchester.

▼ **That seems very sensible.**

(Internal negotiation)

- **I'd like to propose that** we set the price at twenty dollars per unit.

▼ **I have some reservations about that.** If we set the price that high, with the current economic situation, we may price ourselves out of the market.

(Internal negotiation)

- **I suggest that** we produce two separate brochures, one for our operations in the States and another for Europe.

▼ **Perhaps a better idea would be** to have three brochures with two separate ones for England and mainland Europe.

- **I could go along with that.**

BUSINESS SKILLS

(Internal negotiation)

- **I propose that** we should initially employ commission agents in the countries concerned and enter the market that way.
▼ **I think that would be acceptable.**

(External negotiation)

- **We could** give you a discount of ten per cent.
▼ **That doesn't sound very attractive.** We were expecting a much higher discount. We receive twelve per cent from our present supplier.

(External negotiation)

- **We propose that** the guarantee period is extended to two years, instead of the usual one.
▼ **I'm afraid we couldn't agree to that.** It's standard practice to have a one year guarantee period for this type of equipment.

MAKING PROPOSALS

| We propose that... | I'd like to propose that... |
| We could... | I suggest that... |

Making an alternative proposal

Perhaps a better idea would be...

NEGOTIATIONS

REACTING TO A PROPOSAL

Reacting positively	Reacting negatively
That seems very sensible	That doesn't sound very attractive
I could go along with that	I'm afraid we couldn't agree to that
I think that would be acceptable	I have some reservations about that...

Bargaining: linking conditions and offers

- **If you** gave us a long-term contract, **we would** drop the price by two per cent.
- ▼ **Provided that you** start the work immediately, **this is acceptable to us.**

If you made a few modifications, **we could** accept that.

If you guarantee the work for five years, **we are prepared to** accept your offer.

If you give us a bigger discount, **then we will give you** the contract.

If you would be prepared to increase your offer to three million, **we could go along with that.**

If you were prepared to supply the new equipment by the end of February, **we might be able to** increase our offer.

> ### LINKING CONDITIONS TO OFFERS
>
> 1. When we bargain, we link **conditions** to **offers**, so we are **trading**, not just giving something away. It is better to put the condition **before** the offer:
>
>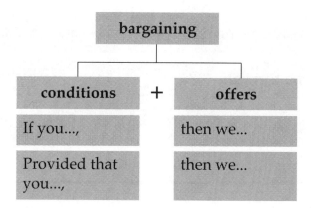
>
> 2. At the start of the bargaining phase, Conditional 2 *(the more tentative conditional)* is often used:
>
>   **If you were prepared to..., we would...**
>
>   When the negotiators are getting nearer to agreement, there is often a change to Conditional 1. *(This is a signal that they are in reach of agreement)*:
>
>   **If you give us..., then we will be able to...**

See also *Conditional* 1 and *Conditional* 2 (Units 15 and 16).

BARGAINING

If you...,

| we would... | we could... |
| we are prepared to... | then we... |

If you would be prepared to...,	we could go along with...
Provided that you...,	this is acceptable to us
If you were prepared to...,	we might be able to...

84 Negotiations: The Final Part

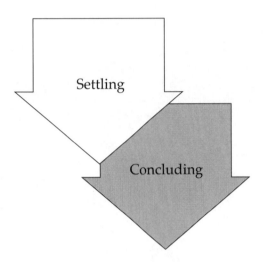

Settling

- If you are prepared to increase your offer by ten per cent, **I think we have a deal.**
- ▼ Yes, I think we could manage that.

- If you guarantee our status as the sole agents and if you can see your way to raising the discount by two per cent, **I think we have an agreement.**
- ▼ All right. I can agree to that.
- We have a deal then.

BUSINESS SKILLS

- **I think we're in reach of an agreement here. The only sticking point is** the time factor. Are you able to complete the work by the end of August?
- Well, we can do that if you will pay for the extra manpower that we'll need in order to meet that deadline.
- I think we could go along with that.
- It's a deal then.

SETTLING

Suggesting a settlement

| I think we are in reach of an agreement here | The only sticking point is... |

| I think we have an agreement |

Confirming the settlement

| All right | I can agree to that |

| I think we have a deal | It's a deal |

| I think we could manage that |

Concluding

Could I just go over what has been agreed? You will start the work at the beginning of January and have it completed by the end of March. **We have agreed to** pay you three million pounds upon completion. **Have I left anything out?**

- **Let's summarise our agreement. You have agreed to** meet all the development costs for the new project. **We will** sub-contract members of our research staff to you for six months. **You will be responsible for** all the day to day expenses of the staff concerned. **Is there anything you'd like to add?**
- ▼ No, **I think you've covered everything. Shall we meet again** at the end of next week to discuss the priorities for the project?

- So, I think we've covered everything. **This is**, of course, **subject to approval by** our Sales Director. I'll consult him as soon as I get back and then **we'll put the agreement in writing**.
- ▼ Fine. **We'll look forward to hearing from you**.

Note
After reaching agreement, it is important to remember to check and summarise everything that has been agreed. This is especially important in an international negotiation, in case there are any misunderstandings.

CONCLUDING

Introducing a conclusion

| Could I just go over what has been agreed? | Let's summarise our agreement |

CONCLUDING

Itemising the details

You will...

We have agreed to...

You have agreed to...

You will be responsible for...

Checking that everything is covered

Have I left anything out?

Is there anything you would like to add?

I think you've covered everything

It is also necessary to agree on any further action (the necessary paperwork, contracts, etc.), and to arrange further meetings if necessary.

FUTURE ACTIONS

Shall we meet again?

Saying what you must do next

This is subject to approval by...

We must put the agreement in writing

Saying that you expect the other person to do something next

We'll look forward to hearing from you

NEGOTIATIONS

85 Letter and E-mail Writing

Salutations and closures

Dear Sir

I am writing in connection with an unpaid invoice of £375 that is owed to us by your company...

Yours faithfully

C.T. Andrews

Dear Ms White

Thank you for your letter of 12th April. I have pleasure in enclosing details of our latest product range...

Yours sincerely

Margaret Spencer

Dear Robert

Thank you very much for the lunch yesterday. It was most enjoyable and I was...

Kind regards

David

SALUTATIONS AND CLOSURES

SALUTATIONS	CLOSURES
A very formal letter Dear Sir Dear Madam Dear Sir or Madam Dear Sirs (when the letter is addressed to a company and not an individual)	Yours faithfully
When you know the person's name Dear Mr Smith Dear Ms Smith Dear Mr and Mrs Smith	Yours sincerely
To someone you know quite well Dear John Dear Angela Dear John and Angela	Best wishes/ Kind regards/ Love (to a good friend)

The above salutations and closures are usual in British English.

*In American English, formal letters often begin with **'Gentlemen'**, and end with **'Sincerely yours'**, **'Yours truly'**, **'Sincerely'**, or **'Yours sincerely'**. **'Yours faithfully'** is not used.*

Useful phrases for business letters

Dear Mr Johnson

[make reference] — **With reference to your letter of** 28 February regarding the possible purchase of software for your accounting systems, [polite phrase] — **we have pleasure in** enclosing details of our spreadsheet programmes.

[recommendation] — **We would recommend that** you consider purchasing the 2XZ package which seems to be the most suitable for your purposes.

[focus attention] — **May we draw your attention to** the fact that there is a special discount on this product during March.

[offer of further assistance] — **If you have any further questions, please do not hesitate to contact us.**

[ending] — **We look forward to hearing from you.**

Yours sincerely

James Benson
Regional Sales Manager

Dear Mrs Tripp

[make reference] — **Thank you for your letter of** 17 July. I should be delighted to send you samples of our products. These will be despatched to you immediately.

I enclose a brochure and price list.

[offer of further assistance] — **Please let me know if I can be of further assistance.**

Yours sincerely

Steven Peacock
Sales Manager

USEFUL PHRASES FOR BUSINESS LETTERS

Making Reference	
With reference to Further to	your letter of (6 September) our telephone conversation, (today) our meeting on (31 March)

...regarding.../...with regard to...
Thank you for your letter of (23 June)

Polite phrases	
We have pleasure in	sending you... enclosing...
We are pleased to	send you... enclose

Focusing attention
May we draw your attention to...

Offering further assistance
If you have any further questions, please do not hesitate to contact us.
We would be pleased to answer any questions that you may have.
Please let me know if I can be of further assistance.

Ending the letter	
We look forward to	hearing from you meeting you on... seeing you on...

WRITING

Business letter layout

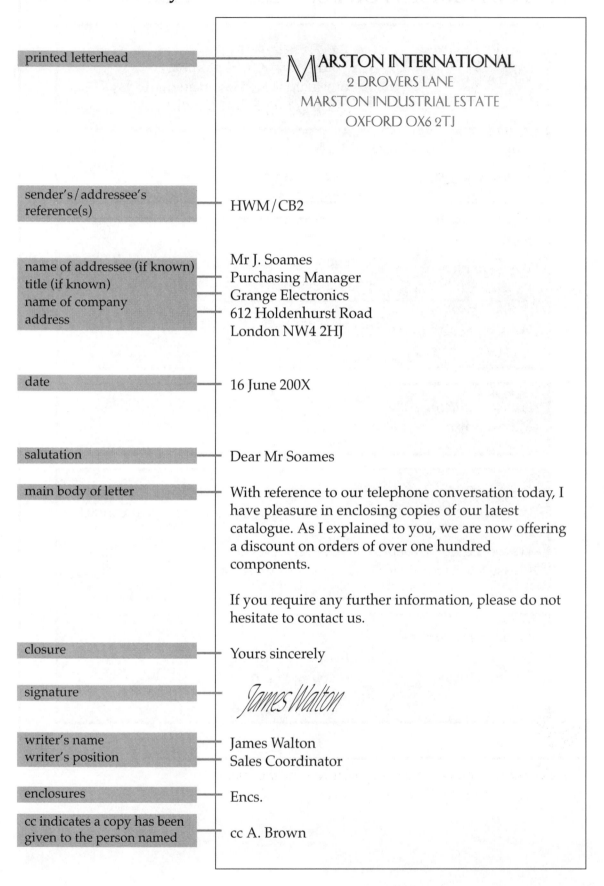

E-mails

Use a **subject line** to help the reader prioritise messages to read.

Use **a salutation.**

Structure
Organise the information to help the reader.

Style
This depends on your relationship with the reader. When responding, use the same level of formality as in the e-mail you received.

Clarity
One idea per paragraph keeps the e-mail 'reader-friendly'.

Tone
Polite and friendly is usually most effective.

Use a **closure**. *Best regards* and *Best wishes* are useful phrases.

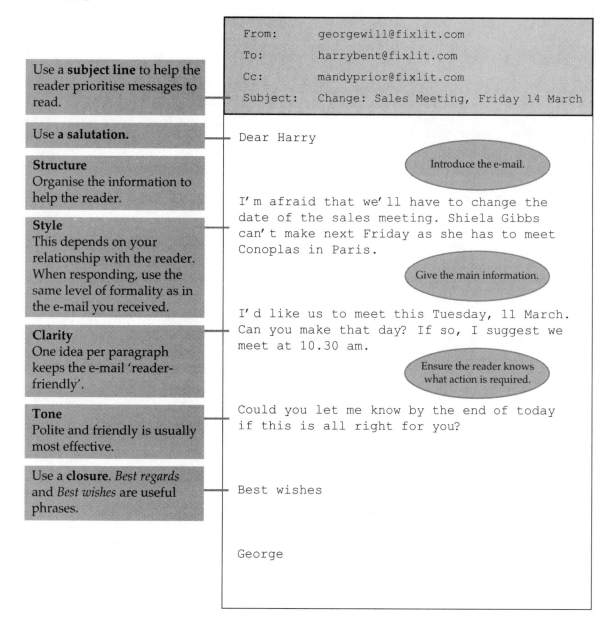

Check your e-mails for accuracy before sending them. Your e-mail should have correct grammar, spelling and punctuation.

86 Form Filling

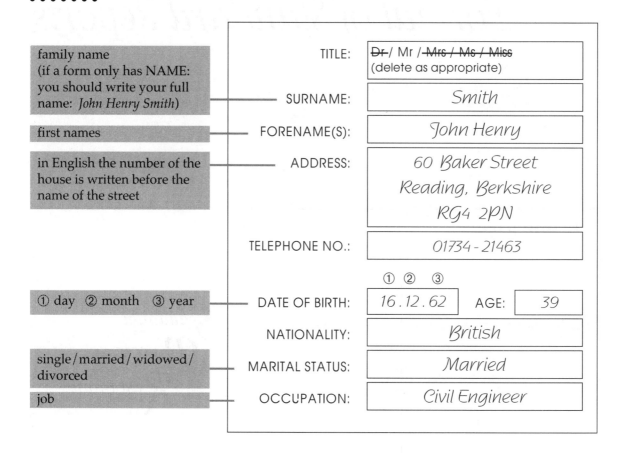

 In American English, the date is usually written like this:
12.16.56 - ① month ② day ③ year

Note
Sometimes you are asked to fill in parts of a form in 'block capitals'. This means you should write like this:

CIVIL ENGINEER, not like this: Civil Engineer.

'Delete' means to cross out:

D̶r̶ / Mr / M̶r̶s̶ / M̶s̶ / M̶i̶s̶s̶

*In British and American English, **'Ms'** can be used for both married and unmarried women and is now very common in written English.*

WRITING

351

87 Report Writing: Format of Standard Reports

The title page

the name of the company	**Sandown Burger Restaurants**
the subject of the report	**Review of Marketing Strategy**
the writer of the report	**K. Clarke** **Group Marketing Manager**
the date of the report	21 June 20XX
reference	Ref. KC/MS 96

Contents list

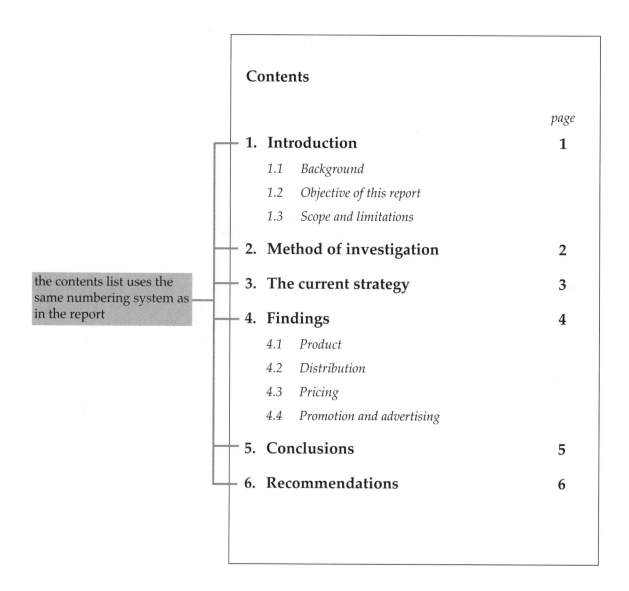

> **Contents**
>
>   *page*

(the contents list uses the same numbering system as in the report)

		page
1.	**Introduction**	**1**
	1.1 *Background*	
	1.2 *Objective of this report*	
	1.3 *Scope and limitations*	
2.	**Method of investigation**	**2**
3.	**The current strategy**	**3**
4.	**Findings**	**4**
	4.1 *Product*	
	4.2 *Distribution*	
	4.3 *Pricing*	
	4.4 *Promotion and advertising*	
5.	**Conclusions**	**5**
6.	**Recommendations**	**6**

Note

1. *Some reports have a brief management summary, setting out the main contents of the report.*

2. *A report to be distributed within a company will have a circulation list stating the names of the people who are to receive the report.*

3. *A report marked* **'confidential'** *must not be shown to anyone else, and the contents must be kept secret.*

WRITING

Introduction

The introduction to a report should explain:

- who has written the report, or what led up to the report *(background)*
- why the report has been written *(objective)*
- what the report covers, and what it does not cover *(scope and limitations)*

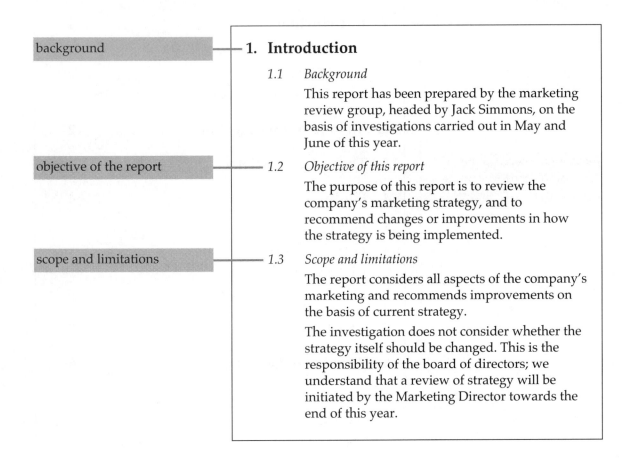

Methods and findings

A report might explain:

- the methods of obtaining information used in the report or presented in the report *(methods of investigation)*
- the situation that the presenter of the report expected to find (in this example this is an explanation of the current marketing strategy)
- the situation that the presenter of the report found *(findings)*

method of investigation or research

2. Methods of investigation

The marketing review group was divided into four teams, which looked at the product, distribution, pricing and promotion respectively.

The investigation was carried out over a four week period in May, by means of discussions with marketing managers at head office and restaurant managers at over fifty locations.

3. The current strategy

The marketing strategy of Sandown Limited for the past three years has been:

- to provide a range of good-quality meals to families, with an emphasis on 'healthy eating'
- to establish a solid market share at existing restaurant locations
- to maintain our image as a chain of reasonably-priced restaurants
- to change our image from fast-food restaurants to restaurants where families can enjoy a relaxed meal together.

The strategy has been implemented by:

- the introduction of a new range of meals, using organically-grown vegetables and fruit
- improving the facilities at existing restaurants, with a $5 million expenditure programme
- reducing prices of main courses, but increasing prices of starter courses and drinks
- promoting the theme of relaxed family eating through television and billboard advertising.

findings

4. Findings

Our investigations produced the following findings:

4.1 Product

Although new meals have been introduced to the menus in restaurants, only a few have been popular with customers. The rest have been sold in only small quantities, and restaurant managers would like to drop unsuccessful items from their menus. They claim that large quantities of unused food are thrown away each week.

4.2 Distribution

The $5 million expenditure programme has been completed. Restaurant managers have expressed their satisfaction with the improvements. Many customers praise the quality of the decor and facilities.

WRITING

> 4.3 *Pricing*
> Over the past three years the prices of main courses have been reduced on average by 20%. Prices of starters have been raised by 25% and drink prices have gone up by 10%. The effect on sales and profits appears to have varied between restaurants. On the whole, restaurants have increased both sales and profits during this time.
>
> 4.4 *Promotion and advertising*
> An extensive advertising campaign is carried out each year. Market research suggests that the image of our restaurants as a place to have relaxed family meals has been recognised by the public.

Concluding and recommending

The main report should end with conclusions or a summary of the findings and (in many reports) recommendations for action to be taken.

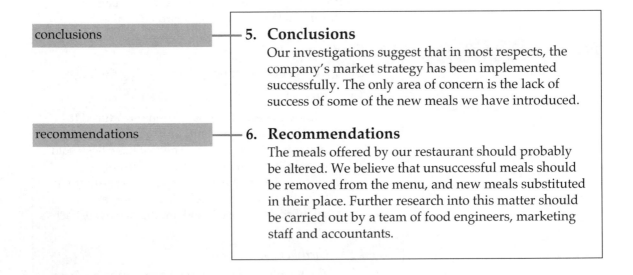

> conclusions — **5. Conclusions**
> Our investigations suggest that in most respects, the company's market strategy has been implemented successfully. The only area of concern is the lack of success of some of the new meals we have introduced.
>
> recommendations — **6. Recommendations**
> The meals offered by our restaurant should probably be altered. We believe that unsuccessful meals should be removed from the menu, and new meals substituted in their place. Further research into this matter should be carried out by a team of food engineers, marketing staff and accountants.

Note

*At the end of many reports, there are **appendices** or **annexes** which provide **additional details** of findings or the results of investigations.*

*There may also be a **bibliography** of references or books consulted, for example, government reports or text books.*

   appendix (i)   appendices (ii, iii, iv...)

   annex (i)   annexes (ii, iii, iv...)

Words at Work

88 Words at Work: Introduction

Business vocabulary

The **Words at Work** section contains useful vocabulary related to various fields of business. The vocabulary is general, not highly specialised. The focus is on the organisation of vocabulary.

Five aspects of vocabulary are dealt with:
- definitions of 'key' words
- word partnerships
- word families
- British and American English
- word stress

Word partnerships

It is helpful to know words that are associated with each other or which are frequently used together. For example, there are a number of words that go with the word **'sales'** to make a **word partnership**: **'sales force'**, **'sales team'**, **'sales representative'**, etc.

Word families

It can also be helpful to see a **word family** together. A word family consists of the noun, verb, adjective, etc. with the same stem:

NOUNS	VERB	ADJECTIVE
competition competitor	(to) compete	competitive

British and American vocabulary

Flags have been used where American words are different from British ones:

   Chairman

   President

Occasionally, British and American word stress is different:

   ○ ● ○ ○
          ad**ver**tisement

   ○ ○ ● ○
          adver**tise**ment

Flags have also been used where spellings differ:

   adviser

   advisor

WORDS AT WORK

Word stress

At the end of each unit, there is a section on **word stress** to help you remember how to pronounce words. **Word stress** has been indicated like this:

● ○ ○
manager

The black dot over **'man'** indicates that **'man'** is the stressed syllable.

○ ● ○
In the word, 'de**part**ment', **'part'** is stressed.

Here are some other examples:

○ ○ ● ○ 　　　　○ ● ○ ○
compe**ti**tion　　　com**pe**titor

89 Companies

Types of company

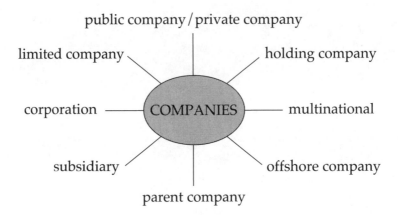

A **subsidiary company** is a company where more than half the shares (voting rights) are owned by another company, the **parent company**, or where the parent company can control who is on the Board of Directors.

The company which owns the subsidiary is called the **parent company**, or the **holding company**.

A **holding company** may own several **subsidiary companies**. The **parent company** and its **subsidiaries** make up a **group of companies**.

A company in which all the capital is owned by the holding company is known as a **wholly-owned subsidiary**.

⚠ Typical Errors	Correct
~~mother company~~ ~~daughter company~~	parent company subsidiary

*In the US, companies are known as **corporations**.*

Company structure

A company (or business unit within a company) may have an organisation structure as shown here:

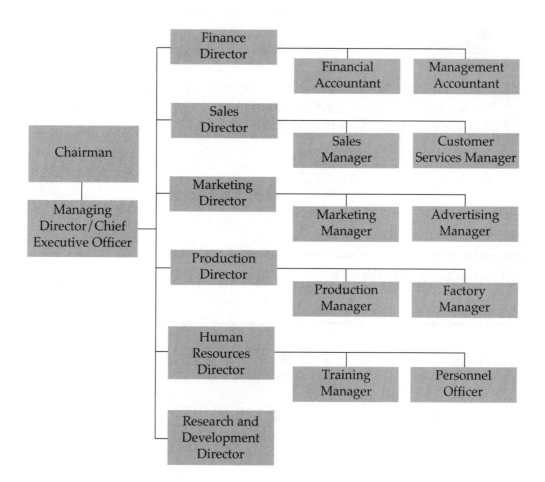

An **executive director** is **responsible for** a particular division or part of the company, for example, the **Finance Director**, **Production Director** and so on. The executive directors (and sometimes, **non-executive directors** as well) together with the **Managing Director** and **Chairman**, make up the **board of directors**. This is the main decision-making body in the company.

Middle managers are **responsible to senior management**. Each department is normally **headed by** a manager who is **in charge of** the department.

Note

When talking about company structure, we often use these phrases:

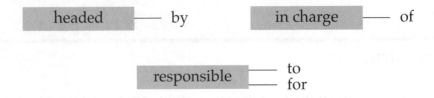

In the US, the Chairman of the Board is known as the **President**. The Managing Director is called the **Senior Vice-President**. Other directors may be called, for example, **Vice President (Production)**.

Companies: word stress

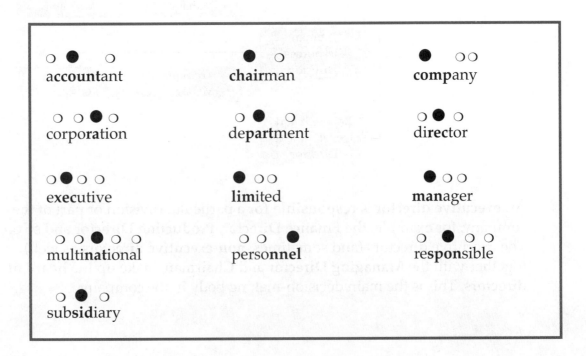

WORDS AT WORK

90 Production

What does production involve?

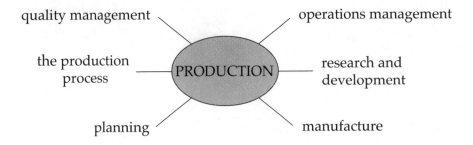

In a manufacturing industry, the term **production management** is used. In a service industry, **operations management** is more common. The **production** or **operations manager** has responsibility for generating and producing the company's products and services.

Manufacture is the making of goods from raw materials.

Computer-aided manufacture is the use of computer-controlled processes to manufacture goods.

Production: word partnerships

The **product life cycle** is the length of time from the introduction of a new product on to the market until its decline and withdrawal.

The **product range** is all the different products manufactured by a company.

The **product mix**, in a company which produces a range of products, is the proportion that the amount of each product bears to the total production/selling quantity.

Quality management

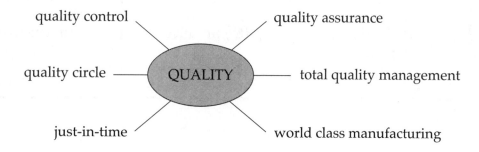

Quality assurance and **quality control** are sometimes confused.

Quality assurance is concerned with all processes and functions to ensure quality from the initial design of a product through the whole production process.

Quality control is an aspect of **quality assurance**. It is a system for checking the quality of materials used and of the finished product, and comparing it with standards set out in the product specification.

A **quality circle** is a group of several employees from the same part of a company who meet regularly to discuss methods of work that affect the quality of the product.

The **total quality management** doctrine stresses the fact that recognition of the customer's needs and demands is vital to a company's success. It also stresses the importance of involving employees in the quality movement and the need for continuous improvement.

Just-in-time (JIT) is a system whose objective is to produce products when they are required by customers, or to buy materials from suppliers when they are required for production. In a JIT system, there should be no requirement to hold stocks of materials or finished products.

World class manufacturing is a term to describe manufacturing excellence. Features of world class manufacturing are total quality management, just-in-time (JIT) systems, and continuous improvement.

Production: word family

NOUNS	VERB	ADJECTIVE
product production productivity producer	(to) produce	productive

Production: word stress

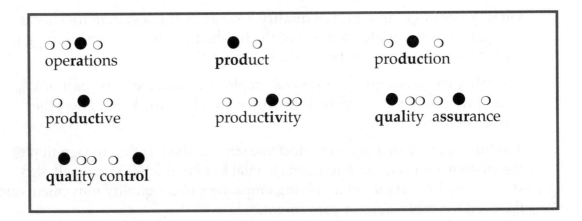

Production time

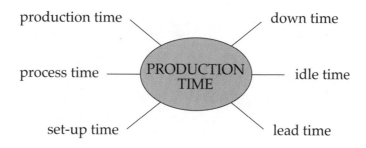

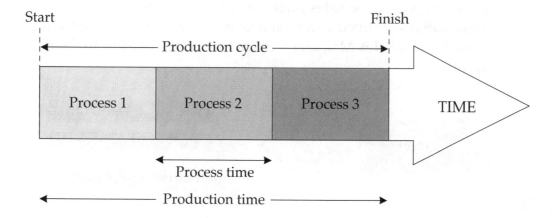

Down time is the period of time when a machine or workstation is out of action due to a functional failure.

Idle time is the period of time when a machine or workstation is available for use, but is not in use.

Set-up time is the period required to prepare equipment before a production activity can begin.

Lead time is the time from the start of an activity to its completion. For example, a **supply lead time** is the time from placing an order with a supplier to delivery of the purchased item.

91 Sales

People in sales: word partnerships

In most companies, the **sales force** consists of a number of **sales representatives** grouped in regional teams (**sales teams**). Each team is responsible to a **Sales Manager** who, in turn, is responsible to the **Sales Director**.

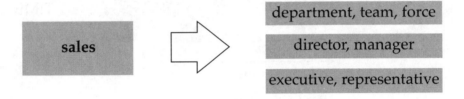

Financial aspects of sales: word partnerships

Our **sales forecast** for this year is £2,000,000.

The **sales figures** for last month were very good.

The **sales budget** seems rather over optimistic as demand is not very high in the winter.

Sales planning: word partnerships

We think that the **sales potential** of the new product is strong. We have decided to mount a big **sales drive**, with an advertising and **sales promotion** campaign. If our sales representatives exceed their **quotas**, they can expect to receive good commission.

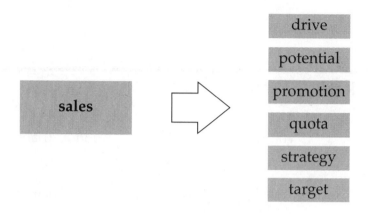

Sales: word stress

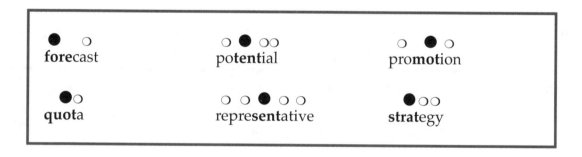

92 Marketing

Types of market

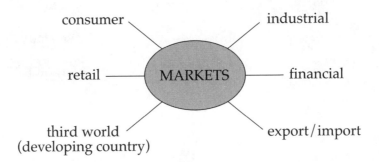

A **retail market** is where the sale of goods is to the **end customer**, that is, goods are sold directly to the customer through a **retailer** rather than through a **wholesaler** who buys from manufacturers and sells to **retailers**.

Market: word partnerships

A **market segment** is a part of a market.

A **market niche** is a small market segment. Some companies focus on a **market niche** for their products. They follow a **niche strategy**, focusing on a **segment** of the market where needs are not being fully met.

Market share is the portion or percentage of a total market held by a company.

Market penetration is the extent to which a company gains a **share** of a market.

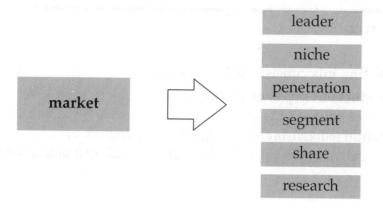

Describing markets

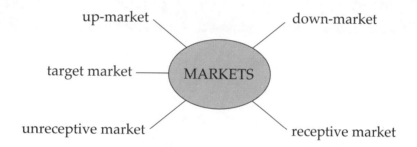

Up-market means the expensive end of the market. We can describe a product as **an up-market product**. (Something that is designed to appeal to people with expensive tastes.)

Down-market means the cheaper end of the market.

The **target market** is the market that the producer is trying to attract.

A **receptive market** is one in which there is already a lot of interest in the product being marketed.

An **unreceptive market** is one which is more difficult to break into.

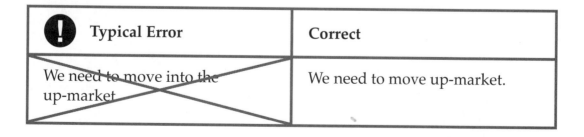

Marketing mix

The **marketing mix** consists of **'the four Ps'**:
- the **product** *(development, design, quality)*,
- **price** *(how much it costs, discounts)*,
- **promotion** *(advertising, publicity, selling activities)*,
- **place** *(how the product will be distributed and where it will be sold).*

Marketing: word stress

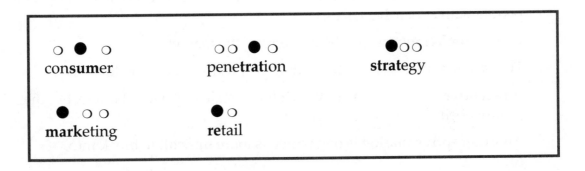

93 Advertising

The aims of advertising

The aims of advertising are to:

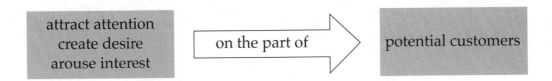

This is done by creating advertisements that **catch the eye**, and also by using memorable **jingles** (short, simple tunes and songs used in television and cinema advertising).

Advertising: word partnerships

An **advertising agency** advises companies on the best way of advertising their products.

An **advertising campaign** is a planned set of advertising operations over a length of time.

Products are often advertised across a wide range of **media** (newspapers, magazines, television commercials, billboards, trade fairs, etc.).

Types of advertising

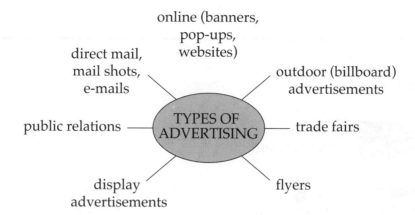

The company may decide to send representatives to **trade fairs** where **display advertisements** will be needed.

A company sometimes sends brochures directly to a potential buyer. This is called **direct mail**.

Sometimes, descriptions of a product are sent to a number of different addresses at the same time. This is called a **mail shot**.

Companies are increasingly investing in **online advertising** on the internet in "paid for" space such as **banners** and **pop-ups** as well as in promotions on company **websites**.

A **flyer** is a leaflet produced for advertising purposes.

Public relations aims to present and preserve an attractive image of a company in the eyes of the public. **Publicity** can be articles in the mass media about a company. This is sometimes seen as **free advertising** but the company has to spend time preparing news releases and encouraging editors to print them.

! Typical Errors	Correct
We placed an announcement in the newspaper.	We placed an **advertisement** in the newspaper

*You do find 'announcements' in newspapers, but they are used to announce births, marriages, deaths, etc. If you want to **sell** something, you place an 'advertisement' in the paper.*

WORDS AT WORK

Advertising: word stress

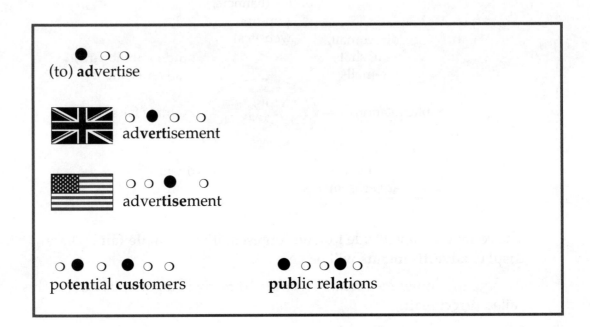

94 Finance

Types of investment

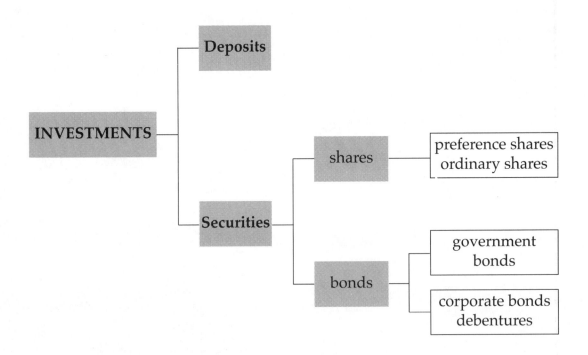

Preference shares yield a fixed dividend.

Ordinary shares are also called **equity shares**.

Ordinary dividends are not fixed but decided by the board of directors. Most public companies pay two dividends each year, an **interim dividend** and a **final dividend**.

Companies might issue bonds, such as **debenture stock**, or **eurobonds**. Bonds usually pay **fixed interest**. Governments also issue bonds to borrow money.

'Gilts' or *'gilt-edged securities'* are UK Government **bonds** and can be sold in the bond market. Some gilts are **indexed** and some carry **variable interest rates**.

In the US, *'**preference stock**'* is used instead of preference shares, and *'**common stock**'* instead of ordinary shares.

'Treasury bonds' or *'Treasuries'* are US government bonds.

Investment: word partnerships

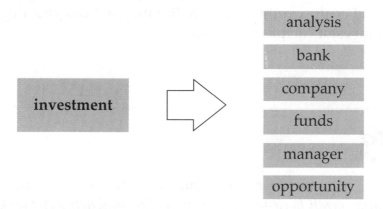

Investment analysis is the forecasting of stock and share prices based on a study of the trading outlook for each company.

An **investment bank** is a financial organisation that alone, or as part of a syndicate, buys a new issue of bonds or stock and sells, in smaller units, to the public.

Investment bankers take over the risk and responsibility for the financial success of the new issue. **Investment bankers** are sometimes called **underwriters**.

Credit: word partnerships

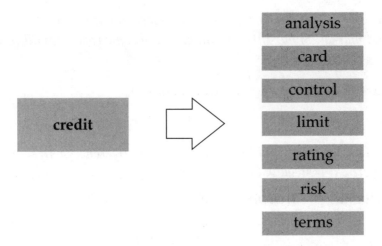

Credit limit is the amount of credit that is allowed by a supplier to a customer. The limit applies to both the value of the goods the customer may have without immediate payment, and the time allowed him to pay.

Credit rating is a system of classifying companies according to their financial strength and credit-worthiness. A credit rating indicates the degree of trust a lender or investor can place in them.

*In the UK, companies have **credit control** departments which are responsible for granting credit to customers, for preventing **bad debts** and for keeping the amount of **overdue debts** as small as possible.*

*In the US, '**credit control**' is action taken by a government, working through the banking system, to control the volume of credit especially the granting of loans and allowing of overdrafts by banks to the public. In the UK, this is called '**monetary control**'.*

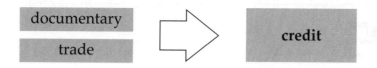

A **documentary credit** is an arrangement between a bank and an importer for settling international commercial transactions.

The bank makes a conditional undertaking to pay the exporter (seller) on behalf of the importer (buyer). The bank will accept bills of exchange drawn by the exporter up to an agreed total amount. The bills must have specified shipping documents and other documents (such as an invoice) with them, otherwise the bank will refuse to pay.

Credit terms are the conditions under which trade credit is given by a supplier to a customer, for example, the time which a supplier gives the customer to pay for goods supplied.

Trade credit is the sale of goods or services on credit. Payment by the customer is due at a time later than delivery of the goods or services.

Taxation: word partnerships

These are the main taxes in the UK:

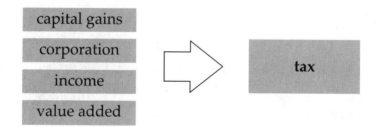

Note
Withholding tax is income tax withheld by law and paid to the government by an employer from an employee's pay or by a bank or other financial institution from interest or dividend paid.

In the UK, 'capital gains tax' is a capital tax charged on a gain resulting from the sale of an asset.

In the US, a gain from the sale of a capital asset is treated as income and is liable to income tax but at a lower rate than that charged on normal income.

Tax evasion is the illegal non-payment of tax.

Tax avoidance is legal non-payment of tax.

When a **tax concession** is given to a company, the normal rules of taxation are not applied. Taxation is either reduced or not charged at all.

A **tax loophole** is a weakness in the **tax law** that creates an opportunity for tax avoidance.

Tax relief is a **tax-free** amount allowed in calculating a taxpayer's **taxable income**.

A **tax haven** is a country where taxation is low.

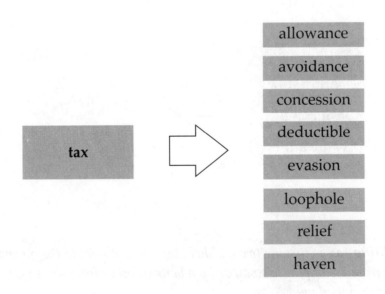

Balance sheet: assets and liabilities

COMPANY
BALANCE SHEET

Assets	$000	$000	Liabilities	$000
Fixed assets			*Current liabilities*	
Land and buildings		1,400	Bank overdraft	50
Machinery		500	Trade creditors	350
Equipment		300	Other creditors	300
		2,200		700
Current assets				
Stocks	700		Bank loan	200
Debtors	490		8% bonds	500
Cash	10			1,400
		1,200	Share capital and reserves	2,000
		3,400		3,400

A **balance sheet** is a financial statement showing the assets, liabilities and capital of a business.

Assets are the items that the business owns or is owed, such as buildings, machinery, equipment, stocks, debtors (amounts receivable) and cash.

Liabilities are amounts of money owed by the business to someone else (creditors), such as bank loans, bonds issued and money owed to suppliers (trade creditors).

Capital represents the owners' stake in the business. In a company, capital consists of share capital and reserves.

stocks
debtors
creditors

inventory
receivables
payables

Profit: word family

NOUNS	VERB	ADJECTIVE	ADVERB
profit profitability	profit (make a profit)	profitable	profitably

A **profitable** business is a business which makes **profit**.

Profitability is the degree to which a business is **profitable**.

Gross profit is sales minus the cost of sales.

Operating profit is **gross profit** minus **operating expenses** or **overheads**.

A **profit and loss account** is an accounting summary which shows the **net profit** of a business before taxation during a given period (typically one year).

Finance: word stress

●○○●
credit con**trol**

○●○
de**ben**ture

○○●○○●○
docu**men**tary **cred**it

○●○
e**va**sion

○●○
in**vest**ment

●○○○
profitable

○○○●○○
profita**bil**ity

○●○○
se**cu**rities

WORDS AT WORK

95 Personnel (Human Resources)

A personnel manager's responsibilities

Personnel management involves the organisation and training of staff.

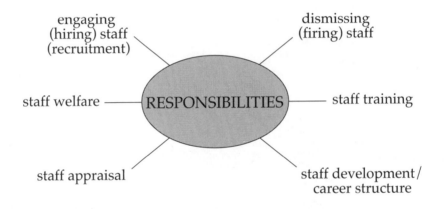

Hiring staff

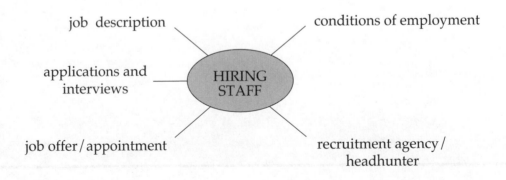

When a **vacancy occurs** in a company, the **Personnel Department** usually prepares a **job description** with an outline of the **conditions of employment**.

The Personnel Department also have to consider the **qualifications, qualities**, and **experience** that are required for the job.

An **advertisement** is usually **placed** in a newspaper or a professional journal.

After the **letters of application** have been received, a **short list** is **drawn up** and **candidates** are invited for **interview**. After one or more interviews, a job **offer** and then an **appointment is made.**

A personnel manager sometimes uses the services of a **recruitment agency**. Staff may also be **headhunted** (recruited by a **headhunter**) who persuades them to leave one company and join another.

In the UK, 'personnel' is commonly used, but many UK companies now use the term 'human resources'.

In the US, 'human resources' is commonly used.

Dismissing staff

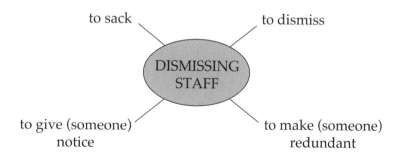

If an employee is not carrying out his/her duties satisfactiorily, or of he/she does something against the company rules (is guilty of **misconduct**), he/she is first given an **oral reprimand**. If there is no improvement, this is followed by a **verbal warning** and, finally, a **written warning**. If there is still no improvement, the company may decide to **dismiss** or **sack** the employee.

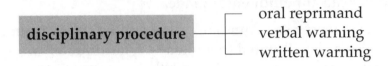

Staff can be made **redundant** or **laid off** if there is no longer work for them.

Fringe benefits

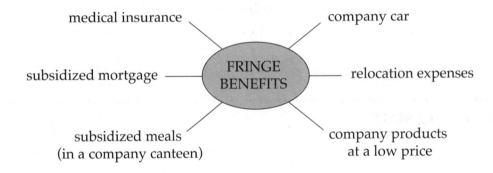

Fringe benefits or **perks** may be given to employees in addition to their normal salaries.

Application: word family

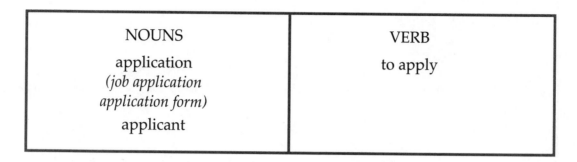

An **applicant** is someone who **applies** for a vacant post.

Personnel: word stress

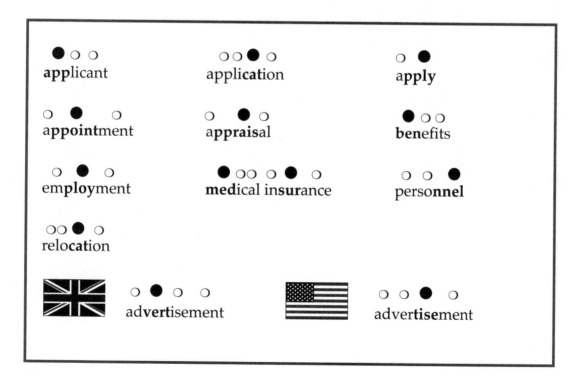

Reference

96 Irregular Verbs

The cost of petrol (rose) last year.
PAST SIMPLE

Prices have (risen) steadily in the last few months.
PAST PARTICIPLE

VERB	PAST SIMPLE	PAST PARTICIPLE
become	became	become
begin	began	begun
blow	blew	blown
break	broke	broken
bring	brought	brought
build	built	built
buy	bought	bought
catch	caught	caught
come	came	come
cost	cost	cost
cut	cut	cut
drink	drank	drunk
drive	drove	driven
eat	ate	eaten
fall	fell	fallen
feel	felt	felt
find	found	found
fly	flew	flown

VERB	PAST SIMPLE	PAST PARTICIPLE
forbid	forbade	forbidden
forget	forgot	forgotten
get	got	got
give	gave	given
go	went	gone
grow	grew	grown
hear	heard	heard
hold	held	held
keep	kept	kept
know	knew	known
leave	left	left
lend	lent	lent
lose	lost	lost
make	made	made
mean	meant	meant
meet	met	met
pay	paid	paid
read	read	read
ring	rang	rung
rise	rose	risen
say	said	said
see	saw	seen
sell	sold	sold
send	sent	sent
show	showed	shown
shut	shut	shut
sink	sank	sunk
sleep	slept	slept
speak	spoke	spoken
stand	stood	stood
take	took	taken
tell	told	told
think	thought	thought
understand	understood	understood
win	won	won
write	wrote	written

REFERENCE

Index

A

a/an	165-166
indefinite article	168, 171
ability	92-93
able to	93, 98
about	148, 330
absolutely	122
acceptable	325, 335
accident (by)	159
accompanied by	102
account	
give an account of	155
accountant	366
active	251
addition	
in addition to	242
address	351
address your remarks	306
adjectives	118, 208
advance (in)	160
advantages	286, 310
advantage in	156
advantage of	155-156
adverbs	120, 208
modifying adjectives	121
modifying adverbs	122
advertisement	378-380, 391, 393
advertising	356, 378
advertising agency	378
advertising campaign	378
media	378
advice	
giving advice	70, 113, 117
listen to	72
advise someone to	76
afford to	74
afraid	
I'm afraid...	226, 295, 335
after	29, 38, 140
day after	199
after that	259, 283
agenda	300, 302, 303, 304, 325
on the agenda	161
ages: comparing	127-128
ago	15, 199
agree	74, 132, 313, 325, 335, 340
agree on	151, 153
agree to	153, 335
agree with	152-153
wouldn't you agree that...?	256
agreed	307
agreed by	110
agreement	327, 340, 341
in agreement	160
all right	226, 229, 231
allow someone to	76
allowed	
not allowed to...	110
almost certainly	50
along	
go along with	334
already	28, 36, 38, 242, 288
also	242
alternative	243
alternatively	242, 310
although	240
always	2, 12, 24, 124-125
am and pm	197
annex	357
announce	14, 132
announcements	379
annually	3
answer	
answer to	156
answer telephone calls	20
answer questions	294, 329
anticipate	254
any	173-175
hardly any	120
with countable nouns	165
with uncountable nouns	166
apologies for absence	301
apologise for	149
apologising	225
appear to	74
appear to be ...ing	77
appear to have	78
appendix	357
application (job)	391, 393
apply	393
apply for/to	113, 149
appointment	
make an appointment	188
appraisal	393
appreciate	
I do appreciate	231
approve of	150
area	283
arrange to	74
arrangements (future)	10
articles	168
as	139
as a rule	255
as... as	126, 140
as long as	61
as soon as	29, 38
as well as	242
assets	387
ask	77, 132, 136-137

ask for permission	226
ask for something	224
ask for views	305
ask someone	
to do something	76, 227
to explain	261
to repeat	261
to translate	261
assure	
I can assure you	296
at	158
attempt to	74
attention	
may I draw your attention to?	99, 346
attitude to	156
available	276
avoid ...ing	81

B

back	
be back	275
come back to	288
go back to	288
bad (not too)	217
bad debts	384
balance sheet	387
banners	379
bar chart	285
barely	121
bargaining	336
be	
be prepared to	336
before	36, 38, 140
the day/week before	135
begin	
begin by	325
shall we begin?	300
begin to	75
begin with	283
believe	5-6
belong to	4-6, 151
benefit	286
fringe benefit	392
best	128-129
best wishes	345
better	129
better idea	334-335
it would be better to/if	256
between	157
bid	
make a bid	44
birth	
date of birth	351
bitterly	121

board of directors	365
bonds	382
boom	247
both	182
bottom out	249
bound to	252, 253
bring	
bring to a close	319
bring to an end	291
budget (sales)	372
buoyant (market)	251
business	
any other business?	308
do business	189
on business	161
by	52, 102, 158
go by car	50
by the time	36
by this time next...	51
bye!	219

C

call back	274, 276
calling	
calling about	271
I'm calling from	267
campaign (advertising)	378
can	84, 92-96
can I/we...?	226, 229
can I help you?	274
can I say something?	314
can I speak to...?	268, 273
can you...?	227
can you tell me...?	330
candidates	20, 391
can't	92-96
can't have	94-96
can't I persuade you to...?	256
capital	387
capital gains tax	386
cash	160
catch	
I didn't quite catch that	261
cause of	155
century	199
certain/certainly	50, 252, 253
certainty	50, 89, 252
chair	301
chairman	301, 365-366
chairperson	301, 326
chance	
any chance of?	226
by chance	159
change	

for a change...	159
make changes	106, 188
changing situations	9
charge	
in charge	26
in charge of	160, 366
chart (pie chart)	285
cheerio!	219
cheque	159
chief executive officer	365
clarification	315, 333
asking for clarification	308
clarifying	294
clause	138, 142
clearer	
make clearer	333
climb to	247
closed question	136
collapse	248
come	
come back to	288
come to you	306
commands	137
commence ...ing	81
common stock	383
company	364, 366
compared with	240
comparing	240
comparison	126, 130
in comparison with	240
there's no comparison between	240
competition	362
competitor	362
complain	132
complain about	148, 152
complain to	151-152
complaint	
make a complaint	188
completely	122
computer-aided manufacture	368
concentrate on	151
concern	
understand your concern	296
conclude by	291
conclusion (in conclusion)	259
conclusions	356
Conditional 0	64, 207
Conditional 1	66, 69, 207, 337
Conditional 2	68, 337
Conditional 3	72, 207
conditions	337
confidence (in confidence)	160
confident (be confident that)	254
confidential	353
confirmation	333
congratulations!	236

connection with	157
consider	287
consider ...ing	81
considerable/considerably	127, 250
consist of	150
consumer	376
contact with/between	26, 157
contain	5
contents	353
contrasting	240
control (under control)	162
corporation	366
correct	
that's correct	331
correcting	333
correctly	
understand correctly	331
cost	4
cost of	155
costs	
at all costs	158
could	84, 92-96
could I/we...?	226
could I have...?	224, 233
could I speak to...?	267
I wondered if you could...?	16
possibility	253
we could...	335
with Conditional 2	71
could you...?	224, 227, 276
could have	94-96
with Conditional 3	73
couldn't have	94-96
countable nouns	164, 168, 170, 176, 178-179, 186-187
course (of course)	226-227
cover everything	342
credit	384
credit card	159
credit control	384, 388
documentary credit	385, 388
credit limit	384
credit rating	384
trade credit	385
creditors	387

D

daily	3
date	198, 348
date of birth	351
date of report	352
days of the week	198
deal	
have a deal	340

it's a deal	341
with	288
dear ...	344
debenture	382, 388
debtors	387
debts	
bad	384
overdue	384
decade	199
decide	
decide on	92
decide to	30, 38, 74
decision	
make a decision	188
reach a decision	72
decimals	201
declare	132, 319
decline	248
decrease	248
definitely (not)	50, 89, 252
degree of change	250
delay	
delay in	154
delay ...ing	81
delete	351
demand for	154
department	268, 366
depend on	4-5, 151, 330
depth of	155
despite	240
did...?	14, 15, 17
didn't have to	106
didn't need to	107, 109
difficulty	
difficulty in	154, 157
difficulty with	157
direct mail	379
direct speech	133-135
director	364-366
disadvantages	286, 310
disadvantages of	155
disagreement	295
discuss with	14, 38
discussion (under)	162
dislike	5
dismiss (staff)	391, 392
display advertisement	379
distribution	355
divide (a talk) into	283
divided by	201
dividends	382
do	189
do/does...?	2-7
documentary credit	385, 388
done (well done)	236
don't have to	106

doubt if/whether	4, 254
doubts (have)	295
down	
down to business	300
down-market	375
downward trends	248
dramatic/dramatically	250
draw	
draw your attention to	346
drop	248

E

each	186-187
either	184-185
elder/eldest	127-128
e-mail	349, 379
employment	393
enable someone to	76
end	
at the end of	161
in the end	160-161
engaged (line)	274
enjoy ...ing	81
entirely	122
equals	201
equity shares	382
evasion (tax)	386
even though	240
ever since	33
every	187
every other day	3
everyone	281
example	
for example	159, 244
excuse me	225, 314
executive	366
executive director	365
expand	247
expect	48, 77, 254
expect to	74
expectation	114
explain	132, 287
extension number	270
extremely	122-123, 284, 312

F

factors	330
fail to	74
faithfully (yours)	344
fall	248
fall in	155
family name	351

far (so far)	28
farewells	219
fast	121-122
faster/fastest	131
favour	286
do someone a favour	189
few/a few	179, 181
figures	285
finally	259, 283, 310
findings	354-355
fine	217
I'm fine	216, 322
that's fine	271
finish ...ing	81
first	
at first glance	158
first names	351
first of all	258, 283
firstly	258, 283, 310, 325
fluctuate	249
follow	
don't follow	316
following (the following)	135
for	27, 32-33, 40-41, 52, 149, 154, 159
for a holiday	161
for example	159, 244
for instance	244
forecast (sales)	372-373
forget	4-5
form	351
forward	346, 347
look forward to	81
fractions	202
free	277
frequently	124
fringe benefits	392
fully	122
further	
any further questions	346
further assistance	346
future (talking about)	46, 54

G

general (in general)	255
gentlemen	345
gerund	75, 80-83, 207
after prepositions	81
gilts	383
give	
to give an example	244
glance	
at first glance	158
go	

go along with	334, 336
go back to	288, 289
go down	248
go out of business	66
go over (again)	308, 318, 342
go up	246, 247
going to	44-46, 54, 67
good	
good idea	313
good to see you (again)	322
good afternoon	268
good evening	219
good morning	216, 266, 280, 300, 322
goodnight	219
gradual(ly)	251
graph	285
great	
that's great news!	236
that would be great	228
greeting	
greeting an audience	280
greetings	216, 322
gross profit	388
growth	247
guess (at a guess)	158

H

had	36-39
had been	
had been ...ing	40-42
passive	56-59
half	202
half past	196-197
hand	
on the one hand	241
on the other hand	241, 310
happy (be happy to)	292
hard	118, 120
harder/hardest	131
hardly	120
hardly ever	124
has/have	26-31
has/have been	
having	32-35
passive	56-59
hate	4-5
hate to	75
have something done	57
have to	103-104
don't/didn't have to...	106
having	141
(completed actions)	82
headhunter	391

hear	5
hear about/from	148
height of	155
hello	217, 221, 266
help	
ask for help	16
offer help	89, 113, 229
hi!	217, 220
highly	122, 284
hiring staff	392
hold	
hold the line	267
holding company	364
holiday	
on/for a holiday	94-95, 161
take a holiday	94
hope	5, 48
hope to	74, 319
how	
how about ...?	230
how about ...ing?	228
how about you?	217
how are things?	217, 324
how are you?	216, 222, 237, 322
how do you do?	221-222
how do you say ...?	261
how interesting!	238
how is everything?	237
how many?	178
how much?	177, 181
how often?	3
human resources	390, 391

I

I'd	
I'd like	224, 233
I'd rather you didn't	226
idea	
better idea	334-335
give me an idea	330
good idea	313
idle time	371
if	60-73, 136, 192, 193
	294, 336
I'll	89
I'm	220
I'm from...	220
I'm sorry	225, 227
I'm sorry to...	237
imagine ...ing	81
implications for	287
important	284, 312, 328-329
impossible	253
in	154, 160

in general	255
in principle	255
in (year)	15
increase	14, 28, 68, 72, 98, 246
increase in	154
indirect speech	133-135
Infinitive	74
inform	132
information	166, 167, 170, 209
insist on	151
instance (for instance)	244
instead of	243
intend to	74
intentions	44
interest	
be in your interest	257
interested/interesting	119, 128, 238
interested in	98
interests	328
internet	379
interrupting	314
interruptions	306
interview	20, 391
introducing	
introducing yourself	220-221, 280
introducing other people	221-223
introduction	
introduction to a report	354
inventory	387
investment	388
investment analysis	383
investment bank	383
invitation	228, 232
invitation to	156
is	
...ing	8-13
being...(passive)	58-59
passive	56-59
issue	328
item (agenda)	303-304

J

journey	
have a good journey	218
talking about	323
just (with present perfect)	28
just-in-time (JIT)	370

K

keen to	328
kind	
it's very kind of you	228-229, 231

kind regards	344
know	4-5, 34, 35
let someone know	193
want to know	136

L

last	4, 15
at last	158
last week/month	31
latest (at the latest)	158
lead time	371
learn to	74
leave out	342
length of	155
less ... than	126
let	
let me	229
let me know if	88, 346
let someone do something	78-79
letterhead	348
level off	249
liabilities	387
like	4-5
I'd like	16, 233
like to	75, 282, 328
like to consider	257
would you like?	232
likely to	252
line (telephone)	267, 274
listen to	72
little/a little	180-181
living	
do for a living	189
long	
as long as	61
stay for long	323
long time	195
look	
look at	103
look for	20
look forward to	81, 218, 342, 346, 347
loss (make a loss)	61, 188
lot/a lot of/lots of	176-177, 181
love	5, 345
I'd love one/some	230
I'd love to	228

M

main	328
make	188
it clearer	332
someone do something	78-79
manage	30, 340
to	74
manager	365-366
managing director	365
manufacture	26, 368
many	178, 181, 209
marital status	351
market	
enter a market	26
market niche	374
market penetration	374
market segment	374
market share	14, 28, 128, 285, 374
marketing	374, 376
mix	376
matters arising	301
may	84, 98-100
may have	100
may I/we	99
may I ask ...?	261
may I have ...?	233
may I introduce ...?	221-222
possibility	253
mean	4-5
do you mean...?	294, 315, 332
mean to	74
what I mean is	315, 332
means	
by all means	226
this means that	243
measure/measurements	4
media	378
medical insurance	392-393
meet (pleased to meet)	221
meeting	
aim of	302
call	302
mention ...ing	81
messages (telephone)	276-277
methods	354-355
might	84, 98-100
possibility	253
with Conditional 2	71
you might like to ...	257
might have	100
with Conditional 3	73
mind	
do you mind?	82, 226, 234
mind + gerund	82
would you mind?	82, 226-227, 234, 294
minus	201
minutes (of a meeting)	301-303
miss ...ing	81
mistake (by mistake)	159
Modal Verbs	67, 84-87, 208

moderate(ly)	127, 250
moment	
at the moment	275
just a moment	268, 272, 306
money	
a little/little money	180
make money	188
much money	177
raise money	190
monthly	3
months of the year	198
more ... than	126, 129-131
morning	
this morning	282
most	
the most ...	128-129, 130-131
move on	287, 304, 325
Ms/Miss/Mrs	351
much	127, 177, 181, 208
so	194
multinational	366
multiplied by	201
must	84, 102-105
that must be	104
that must have been	105
mustn't	110

N

name	352
company name	352
my name is	220, 267-268, 280
nearly always	124
need	5, 296
didn't need to	107, 109
need for	154
needn't	106
needn't have	108-109
neither	183-184
net profit	388
never	2, 24, 124-125
news	236-237
next	259, 319
next week/year	135, 199
nice	
nice meeting you	218
that would be very nice	228
nice to meet you	221
nice to see you	217-219
niche (market)	374
no, I'm sorry	224
normally	255
not	
not at all	226
not in	277
not only..., also	242
not too bad	217
notice	
give notice	391
notify	132
numbers	
saying numbers	201

O

object to	151
objections	
no objections	313
raise objections	190
objectives	
objectives of a report	354
obligation	102-103, 116
occasionally	124
occupation	351
o'clock	196-197
of	150, 155
of course (not)	226-227
offer	
offer a discount	61
offer assistance	346
make an offer	188
offer something	230
offers	113, 232, 337
often	2, 24, 123-125
older	
older than ...	127
on	151, 161
on the whole	255
once	
once a year/day	3
at once	158
online	379
open questions	136
opening remarks	300
operating expenses	388
operations	370
operations manager	368
opinion	4
in (my) opinion	160
opinion of	155
options	242, 311
ordinary shares	382
other	
in other words	243
ought to	84, 116-117, 252
ought to have	116
outline	
of a talk	282
overheads	388
own	5-6

P

parent company	364
Passive	56
pay	
pay by	158
pay for	149
pay in	160-161
payables	387
peak	246
penetration (market)	376
per cent	202
perceptions	4
permission	94, 99, 226
not permitted	110
personnel	366, 390, 393
persuade	256
persuade someone to	76
phone	
phone for someone	112
phone to say that ...	29
pick up	61, 95, 247
pie chart	285
pity (what a pity)	239
plan to	74
plans	44
make plans	188
please (yes, please)	230
pleased	
pleased to meet you	221-222
we'd be pleased if	228
pleasure	
it's a pleasure	231
we have pleasure in	348
point(s)	288, 295, 303, 306, 310
adding extra points	242
decimal point	201
main points	290
making a point	311
next point	287
the second point	258
pop-ups	379
possible	253
possible options	242
would it be possible to?	226
possibility	93, 98, 253, 310
possibly	50, 253
could I possibly...?	226
postpone ...ing	81
practice (in practice)	160
practise ...ing	81
predicting	44, 48
prefer	5
preference shares	382
prepare for	149
prepared	
be prepared to...	338
Present Simple	2
contrast with Present Continuous	11
Present Continuous	8
Present Perfect or Past	30-31
president	366
pretend to be ...ing	77
previous	
the previous day/month	135
price	356, 376
raise	190
saying prices	202
principle (in principle)	160, 257
priority	328
probably	50, 123, 252-253
problem	310
procedure	325
process time	371
produce	3
product	355, 376, 370, 378
life cycle	368
mix	369
range	368
production	368, 370
cycle	371
manager	368
time	371
productive	370
productivity	370
profit	388
increase profit	72
make a profit	188
profit and loss account	388
profitability	388
progress	
make progress	188
prohibition	110
promotion (sales)	356, 373, 376
propose	334-335
provided that	61, 338
providing	61
potential (sales)	373
public relations	379-380
purpose of	282
purpose of a meeting	302
put through	268-270

Q

quality	
quality assurance	369-370
quality circle	369

quality control	369-370
quality management	369
quantity	176
quarter	202
quarter to/past	196-197
question(s)	331
answer a question	294-296
clarifying questions	294
closed questions	136
deal with questions	294
inviting questions	292
open questions	136
repeat questions	294
rhetorical question	287, 288
understand	294
quite	122
quite right	332
quota (sales)	373

R

raise	190-191
rapid(ly)	250-251
rapport (establish)	322-325
rarely	124-125
rate of	155
rather	122-123
I'd rather	226
reach	246
reactions	
inviting reactions	305
negative reactions	313, 314, 336
positive reactions	312, 313, 314, 336
reactions to ...	156
reactions to a proposal	336
realise	34
really	121-122
I really must...	225
I'd really like to...	228
really?	238
reason for	154, 287, 326
recall	
recall...ing	81
recap	332
receivables	387
recently (present perfect)	28
recommending	257, 346, 356
I/we recommend that	76
recover	247
recruitment	391
redundant	391-392
make redundant	188
refer forwards/back	288, 289
reference	
with reference to	346

refuse to	74
regards	
give regards	324
kind regards	344, 345
regret (to)	75
relationship with/between	157
relative clause	142, 209
relatively	240
relocation	392-393
rely on	151
remain stable	249
remarks	
opening remarks	300-301
remember (to)	4-6, 75
remind someone to	76
repeat	
could you repeat that?	261
reply	132
reply to	151, 156
report	132
report to	3
representative (sales)	374-375
request	16, 88, 136, 224
require	5
reservations	
have reservations about	334
responsible	342, 366
respect for	154
respond to	152
result	
result in	66
result of	155
retail	376
retail market	374
return (a call)	277
review (under review)	162
right	
all right?	340
am I right?	331
it's all right	229
not quite right	334
that's all right	231
that will be all right	226
rise	190, 246-247
rise by	190
risk ...ing	81
routines	2
rule	
as a rule	255
run through	291, 316

S

sack	391
sales	372
sales	

sales promotion	356, 373, 376	as soon as	29, 38
sales representative	372-373, 375	sorry	225, 227, 261, 275-276, 313-316
sales turnover	14		
salutation	344-345, 348	I'm sorry to	237
say	132	sorry?	261
are you saying...?	315-316	sounds	
say something about	305	that sounds...	336
that is to say...	243	speak	
schedules	6, 46, 54	speak about ...	282
scope		speak more slowly	261
scope of a report	353, 354	to speak	29, 116, 269
seasons of the year	198	to speak to someone about...	272-273
secondly	283, 311	speed of	155
securities	382-383, 388	speed of change	250-251
see	5	spite	
see someone about ...	29	in spite of	240
see to...	103	stable/stability	249, 251
see you again soon	219	stage	
seem	4-5, 336	at this stage	291
seem to	74	stagnant	251
seem to be ...ing	77	stand at/stood at	249
seem to have...	78	start	
segment (market)	374-375	start to	75
sensible (seem)	336	to start with	258-259
sequencing	311, 326	we'll start with	258-259
serious	118	state	132
set an agenda	325-326	state interests	328-329
settling	340-341	states	4-5
set-up time	371	stative verbs	5
shaking hands	223	steady/steadily	250-251
shall	84, 89-90, 112-115	stick to	306
shall I?	89, 112-113, 115, 229	stock	387
shame (what a shame)	237	stop (to)	75
share (market)	14, 28, 128, 285, 374	strategy (sales)	373
shares	382	strongly recommend	257
sharp(ly)	250	subject	
should	84, 112-115, 252	subject line	349
should have	114	subject of a report	352
you should ...	257	subject to ...	342
significant(ly)	118, 120, 127, 250, 286	subsidiary company	168, 364, 366
since	27, 32-33, 140	substantial(ly)	118, 120, 127, 191, 250
sincerely (yours)	346	such	194-195
slightly	121, 127, 250	such ... that	195
sluggish	251	sudden(ly)	250
slump	248	suggest	132, 257, 326, 334
small talk	325	suggest ...ing	81
so	194	suggestions	112
so far	28	make a suggestion	99
so that	194	sum up	29
solution to (a problem)	156	summarising	290-291, 318, 342
some	172-173	superlatives	128, 130
some other time perhaps	228, 237	supply	
with countable nouns	164, 165, 167	supply lead time	371
with uncountable nouns	165-167	supply with	152-153
sometimes	2, 24, 124	suppose	5
soon			

sure	226
I'm not sure if/whether	261
surely	256
surprised	
be surprised to	119
I'd be surprised if	254
surprising	119

T

table (of figures)	285
talk	
talk about	281-283
small talk	325
target market	375
tax	
tax avoidance	386
tax concession	386
tax evasion	386
tax haven	386
tax loophole	386
raise tax	190
tax relief	386
taxation	385
telephone	
make a telephone call	189
on the telephone	161
tell	88, 132, 137, 276
terrible (news)	236
terribly sorry	122
than	126
thank someone for	116
thank you	228-231, 291, 300-301
thank you for your letter	346
thank you very much	228-229, 231
thanks	228-229, 231
that	142, 145
after that	259, 283
that is to say	243
the	
definite article	169, 171
with superlatives	128, 130
then	259, 283, 325, 336-337
theory (in theory)	160
there	
is ... there?	267
think	4-5, 48, 318-319, 330, 332, 341
think about	72, 88, 148, 150
I think you should	257
think of	150
third	202
this is ...	222
though	
even though	240
time	
a little/little time	180
a long time ago	15
by the time	36
clauses	138
in ... days' time	199
in time	160-161
in time for	66
it's time	17
it's high time	17
on time	161
phrases	15, 135
some other time	228, 237
such a long time ago	195
telling the time	196
this time next week	51
times	
three times a day	3
title	268, 348, 351
title page	353
to	151-152, 156
today	281-282, 302
tomorrow	199
topic	287
changing topic	287
total quality management	369
totally unacceptable	284
trade credit	385
trade fair	379
Treasuries	383
trends	246
trouble	
be in (serious) trouble	95
truly (yours)	345
try ...ing something	113
turnover (sales)	14

U

uncountable nouns	165-167, 170, 176-177, 180
under	162
understand	4-5, 34
underwriters	385
unless	61
unlikely	252-253
until	29, 38
up to now	28
up-market	377
upward trends	190-191, 246-247
used to	22-24
be used to ...ing	23, 81
usually	2, 24, 124-125

V

vacancy (job)	390
very	122
very few	179
very well	216
vice-president	366
views on	305
visuals	285
vital/vitally	328-329
voting (at a meeting)	307

W

wait for	32, 40, 149
want	77
want to	4-5, 16
want to know if/whether	136
warn	137
was/were	
being (passive)	58-59
...ing	18-21
passive	56-59
way	
way of doing something	155
under way	162
websites	379
week	
this/last/next week	199
weekly	3
weigh	4
weight of	155
welcome	280-281, 300-301
you're welcome	231
well	120, 123
as well as	242
well done!	236
very well	216
were	
if I were you	70
what	
what a shame	237
what about ...?	230
when	15, 19, 29, 38, 192
when or if?	61, 192-193
whenever	139
whereas	241
whether	136
which	142-143, 145
while	20, 139, 241
who/whom/whose	142-144
whole	
on the whole	255
why don't you...?	228

will	46, 48-54, 66-67, 84, 88-90
will be ...ing	51
will have done	52, 53
wise	
you'd be wise to	256
wish	16, 72
with	152-153, 157
withholding tax	385
world class manufacturing	370
wonder if	16, 329
won't	48-54
words	
in other words	243
work	
work as	26
work for	22, 40, 53
to do work	189
will it work?	48
worries (have no)	296, 330, 331
worry about	107-108
worse/worst	128-129
would	23-24, 39, 68-71, 84, 88-90
certainty	252
would it be possible to...?	226
would like to ...	330
we would ...	338
would you ...?	227, 278
would you like ...?	230, 232
would you like to ...?	228
would you mind ...ing?	227, 234
would have	
Conditional 3	72-73
wouldn't you agree?	256
writing (in writing)	160

Y

years	
saying the years	199
yearly	3
yes, certainly	224, 227
yes of course	224, 227
yesterday	15, 31, 199
yours	
yours faithfully	344-345
yours sincerely	344-346

Z

zero article	170-171

Linguarama International

Linguarama is an international organisation with more than 20 centres in six countries. Each centre teaches a wide range of languages to the highest standards. For advice and information on language training please contact one of the Linguarama centres below or e-mail us at info@linguarama.com.

UK

Linguarama
New London Bridge House
Floor 12a
25 London Bridge Street
London SE1 9ST

Tel: (020) 7939 3200
Fax: (020) 7939 3230

Linguarama
Cheney Court
Ditteridge
Box, Corsham
Wiltshire SN13 8QF

Tel: (01225) 743557
Fax: (01225) 743916

Linguarama
1 Elm Court
Arden Street
Stratford-upon-Avon
Warwickshire CV37 6PA

Tel: (01789) 296535
Fax: (01789) 266462

DEUTSCHLAND

Linguarama Deutschland
Linguarama-Haus
Goetheplatz 2
60311 Frankfurt/Main

Tel: (069) 28 02 46
Fax: (069) 28 05 56

Linguarama Deutschland
Steinstrasse 30
40210 Düsseldorf

Tel: (0211) 867 69 90
Fax: (0211) 13 20 85

Linguarama Deutschland
Marzellenstr 3-5
50667 Köln

Tel: (0221) 16 09 90
Fax: (0221) 16 09 966

Linguarama Deutschland
Rindermarkt 16
80331 München

Tel: (089) 260 70 40
Fax: (089) 260 98 84

Linguarama Deutschland
Friedrichstrasse 60
10117 Berlin

Tel: (030) 203 00 50
Fax: (030) 203 00 515

Linguarama Deutschland
Hopfenburg
Hopfensack 19
20457 Hamburg

Tel: (040) 33 50 97
Fax: (040) 32 46 09

Linguarama Deutschland
Lipsia-Haus
Barfussgässchen 12
04109 Leipzig

Tel: (0341) 213 14 64
Fax: (0341) 213 14 82

Linguarama Deutschland
Leuschnerstrasse 3
70174 Stuttgart

Tel: (0711) 99 79 93 30
Fax: (0711) 99 79 93 44

NEDERLAND

Linguarama Nederland
Arlandaweg 10-28
1043 EW Amsterdam

Tel: (020) 428 05 28
Fax: (020) 428 06 28

Linguarama Nederland
Bleijenburg 1
2511 VC Den Haag

Tel: (070) 364 58 38
Fax: (070) 365 43 81

Linguarama Nederland
Amersfoortsestraat 18
3769 AR Soesterberg

Tel: (0346) 33 25 75
Fax: (0346) 33 25 79

ITALIA

Linguarama Italia
Via S. Tomaso 2
20121 Milano
Tel: 02 89 01 16 66
Fax: 02 89 01 16 52

Linguarama Italia
Via Tevere 48
00198 Roma
Tel: 06 85 35 57 07
Fax: 06 85 35 57 13

Linguarama Italia
Via E. de Sonnaz 17
10121 Torino
Tel: 011 562 03 35
Fax: 011 562 21 63

ESPAÑA

Linguarama Ibérica
Edificio Iberia Mart II
Orense 34
28020 Madrid

Tel: 91 555 04 85
Fax: 91 555 09 59

Linguarama Ibérica
Edificios Trade
Torre Norte
Gran Vía de Carlos III 98-2º
08028 Barcelona

Tel: 93 330 16 87
Fax: 93 330 80 13

FRANCE

Linguarama France
7e Etage, Tour Eve
La Défense 9
92806 Puteaux Cedex
Paris
Tel: (01) 47 73 00 95
Fax: (01) 47 73 86 04

Linguarama France
Tour Crédit Lyonnais
129 rue Servient
69326 Lyon Cedex 03

Tel: (04) 78 63 69 69
Fax: (04) 78 63 69 65

Visit our web-site at http://www.linguarama.com